Margaret Powell was born in 1907 in Hove, and left school at the age of 13 to start working. At 14, she got a job in a hotel laundry room, and a year later went into service as a kitchen-maid, eventually progressing to the position of cook, before marrying a milkman called Albert. In 1968 the first volume of her memoirs, *Below Stairs*, was published to instant success and turned her into a celebrity. She followed this up with *Climbing the Stairs*, *The Treasure Upstairs* and *The Margaret Powell Cookery Book*. She also co-authored three novels, tie-ins to the television series *Beryl's Lot*, which was based on her life story. She died in 1984.

Praise for Margaret Powell

'Anyone who enjoyed *Downton Abbey* or *Upstairs Downstairs* will relish this feisty memoir'

Dame Eileen Atkins

'A nurse worked hard, but a skivvy worked harder – brought to life in this wonderful book'

Jennifer Worth, author of *Call the Midwife*

'Margaret Powell was the first person outside my family to introduce me to that world . . . where servants and their employers would live their vividly different lives under one roof. Her memories, funny and poignant, angry and charming, haunted me until, many years later, I made my own attempts to capture those people for the camera. I certainly owe her a great debt'

Julian Fellowes, creator of *Downton Abbey*

Also by Margaret Powell

Below Stairs

Climbing the Stairs

PAN BOOKS

First published 1969 by Peter Davies Ltd

First published in paperback 1971 by Pan Books

This edition published 2011 by Pan Books
an imprint of Pan Macmillan, a division of Macmillan Publishers Limited
Pan Macmillan, 20 New Wharf Road, London NI 9RR
Basingstoke and Oxford
Associated companies throughout the world
www.panmacmillan.com

ISBN 978-1-4472-1859-3

1 3 5 7 9 8 6 4 2

A CIP catalogue record for this book is available from
the British Library.

Typeset by CPI Typesetting
Printed and bound by CPI Group (UK) Ltd, Croydon, CR0 4YY

Visit **www.panmacmillan.com** to read more about all our books and
to buy them. You will also find features, author interviews and
news of any author events, and you can sign up for e-newsletters
so that you're always first to hear about our new releases.

To my husband, with love

Introduction

IT'S DIFFICULT FOR people to realize the social and financial changes that have taken place since the 1920s – it seems such a short time ago.

When I tell people what it was like when I went into service in 1923, at first they say, 'How awful for you.' Then it suddenly strikes them that it wasn't very long ago, and they think you're exaggerating, that it wasn't like that, that either you had very bad places to work in or that you've made it out to be a lot worse than it was. But in fact there have been vast changes since then.

I think what people fail to understand is that although the status of domestic servants has really risen so dramatically, the real reason for the change is the scarcity of domestic servants nowadays. If they were ten a penny as they used to be they'd be treated in the same way as we were. This goes for other workers, too. I don't think people have changed; it's events that have altered their attitudes.

When I went into service the very name 'service' meant

that you'd said goodbye to all personal freedom – the same as it did for men in the Army, the Navy and the Air Force. Like domestic service, these services used to be filled from the ranks of the uneducated and untrained.

Then there were few jobs open to ill-educated girls. Chances for women were coming, I know, but they were for women who'd had an education – whose parents had either been enlightened and had seen that they were educated as well as the boys, or for women who from the moment that they could get hold of their own money had made sure that they educated themselves.

Most of the people I worked for sprang from the middle classes who, when they acquired wealth and rose in the world, adopted all the social standards of the upper classes.

And the upper classes regarded the state of the poor as inevitable. We were always with them and so long as you didn't attempt to rise in the world – so long as you knew the state you'd been called to – they were even prepared to be gracious and benevolent towards you. So long as they knew that you knew that they were being gracious and benevolent.

I think that they had the same feelings about servants then as wealthy people have now about their possessions – their homes, their cars and all the gadgets that make life worth living. These things need looking after. They don't want them to wear out too quickly, but if they go wrong or become tiresome they can be replaced.

Servants were not real people with minds and feelings. They were possessions.

Since my book *Below Stairs* was published I've had a number of letters from people who were irate that I wrote in the way I did. They said that their mothers always looked after the servants. A number of older people have said also that they thought about their servants' comfort and saw that they had a nice room.

Yes, I agree; perhaps they did. But they still looked on their servants as their possessions. The servants must never have a life of their own. The employers were entitled to say to their servants, 'Oh, what did you do on your day off? Where did you go? Who did you go out with?' And to expect a truthful reply. But if you were to say to *them*, 'And what did you do when you were out last night? Did you have a good evening?' they would have been horrified. You couldn't ask such a thing; you had no right.

When I was reading history for my 'A' levels recently I discovered that even Disraeli, and he was supposed to have been a Liberal, said that there were two nations. And he meant the rich and the poor.

Well there were two nations when I was fifteen, and now I'm sixty-one I still think that there are two nations in this country, even though things are so much better. Just give us a period of high unemployment and you'll see what I mean.

Another great change that there's been is in fashions. When I first went into domestic service, there weren't the facilities that there are now to buy cheap, but good, ready-made clothes.

Now a lot of the well-to-do openly boast that they buy

things from Marks & Spencer or shops like that – buy them ready-made. It's quite the done thing nowadays. But it wasn't the done thing in those days.

Then they had everything made for them. We used to make our own (and they looked like it), because bought ready-made clothes were so expensive.

Of course we used to try to copy the styles of the rich and the people that we worked for. And I often used to think that it was we servants who really changed the fashions. Because as soon as we copied or made anything that looked remotely like what they were wearing upstairs they would discard it and get their dressmaker to design something else. Probably we flattered ourselves; perhaps they would have discarded it in any case.

Mind you, this gap that there was was also something to do with being young, because no matter whatever your status in life then, whether you were working, middle, or upper class, no young people were of any importance.

We were never known as teenagers. We were just young – too young to know anything about business or politics or even living our own lives. All we were expected to do was to keep quiet, take advice and let those who had experience and know-how get on with it.

It didn't just apply to the lower classes. It applied to the well-to-do just the same. Young people's opinions were not consulted and weren't expected to be given either without being asked for. They were learning, and when you're learning you can't advise because you don't know. And that applied to all strata of society.

Nowadays everything's geared to young people. Vast sums are made by firms like the clothing, cosmetics, records, and magazine manufacturers. They make fortunes out of young people. So if these firms are basing their commercial structure on supplying young people with the material things – and if the Government is spending great sums in providing the facilities and opportunities for education – then we shouldn't be surprised at the type of young people that results.

It's no good us crying 'enough, enough' when youth gets up and tells us how they want to see the world run. Because we've made them like that. We've made them important.

But when I look back on my life – although the working-class people of my generation had to work hard for a living – I don't envy young people at all today.

It may seem that they've got everything – material things and freedom to live their lives in the way they want to – but they've also got the urge and the anxiety of wanting to improve the world; as for us, we only wanted to improve ourselves.

Margaret Powell, 1970

1

I WAS THREE days in my first place in London before I had a chance to go out. I arrived there on a Wednesday and as a Wednesday was to be my one afternoon and evening off in the week obviously I didn't get it that week, so my first time out was on the Sunday. I was allowed from three o'clock till ten o'clock every other Sunday, but that first day it took me so long to do all the washing up that I didn't get away until four.

I'd had a letter from my mother the day before – the Saturday. Mother must have sat down and written it the minute I left home, saying that I was to be very careful indeed; everybody knew what London was like. Not actually stating anything definite – kind of innuendoes. Anybody would have thought I was some sort of raving beauty and that every man who looked at me was going to make advances. Instead, what I was in those days was fattish, on the plain side with big hands and bigger feet, and with these poor ingredients I didn't know how to make the best of myself – I don't think many working girls did. At the end of her letter my mother put 'and don't talk to any strangers'. Well, since I didn't know a soul in London if I didn't talk to strangers I wouldn't talk to anyone. So it looked as if I would have to be dumb for the rest of my stay.

Anyway there I was, all ready at four o'clock to go out and I was mad to go and see Hyde Park because it was a place I had read about with its soapbox orators and the guardsmen in their red coats walking around. I asked the cook what number bus to get on because I didn't want to look like some provincial hick that had just come up to London and didn't know anything. I was going to ask for Hyde Park, hand over the right money and look as if I knew it all.

I got on the bus that she told me and I went upstairs right to the front so that I could see everything. I sat there for ages looking all round and very soon it struck me that the buildings were much the same kind that you might see anywhere. But of course being as they were in London I thought, oh well, they must be marvellous.

No conductor took my fare. One came up several times but he never reached the front of the bus. I sat on and on looking. I thought it seemed a long way but I had no idea where things were. Then I could see that we were in a very seedy neighbourhood: dirty little shops, a very slummy place – far more slummy than some of the places around my home.

Before I could do anything about it the conductor came up and said, 'This is the terminus.' So I said, 'I haven't seen Hyde Park yet.' And he said, 'No, you bloody well won't see it on this bus either. You're going in the wrong direction.' 'But this is the right number,' I said. 'Yes,' he said, 'this is the right number but you're going the wrong way. You got on on the wrong side of the road.' 'Well, why didn't you come up and get my fare – why didn't you tell me?' So he said, 'You try being a conductor on a ruddy London bus, and see if you're going to tell people who don't know where they're going where they should be going.'

I got off the bus very crestfallen and not knowing what to do at all. So he said to me, 'Where did you want to go?' I told him I wanted to go to Hyde Park and also that it was my first time in London. So he said, 'What are you going to do now, then?' He thought for a moment. 'I'll tell you what,' he says. 'We'll be going back in twenty minutes. We're going over the café to have a cup of tea and that – why don't you come over with us.' Well, I wouldn't have dreamed of doing a thing like that at home. Not only might someone you know see you but, I mean, it just wasn't done. But after all was said and done I'd gone to London to have an adventurous life so I thought, 'Well, here goes,' and walked over to the café with him and the bus driver.

It was obviously a working men's café full of lorry drivers and bus crews. I was the only member of my sex but nobody seemed to show any surprise at seeing me, so I assumed that they often took women in there.

The bus conductor – I found out that his name was Perce – said, 'Well, sit down.' And we did, at a table that was covered in American cloth and innumerable flies, and he went to get cups of tea for us. That tea! It was so black. What they did was to stick soda in the tea urn – it's a well known trick at these working-class cafés – to get all the colour out of the leaves and make it look strong. And he brought us cakes about the size of tennis balls and the same consistency, too.

Anyway we got talking and this Perce – of course his real name was Percival – told me he lived at a place called the Elephant and Castle. So I said, 'How did it get that name?' 'Oh, well,' he said, 'originally it was called The Castle after the pub there but the landlord's wife got so fat drinking all the stock that they called it The Elephant and Castle.' Green though I was I didn't believe a word of it but I dutifully laughed.

The bus driver, Bert, was a mournful, cadaverous-looking creature and he spoke in such a resigned tone of voice that you felt he'd eaten life's troubled apple, core and all, and all that was left for him was a gradual descent to the grave. Part of his trouble was that he suffered from gastric ulcers. These he told me were rife among bus drivers because of the shift work and the irregular hours they had to do. This and the fact that they couldn't stop the bus often enough to empty their bladders. So they got these gastric ulcers. He reckoned they should have been paid danger money. He may have been right but it's my opinion they got their ulcers from drinking that black tea and eating all those rubbery cakes.

Anyway when I'd got to know him a bit more I found he was a non-stop talker. He showed me photos he'd had taken when he was young and healthy. Apparently he used to go boxing on a Saturday night to earn himself a bit – in the boxing booths, and he told me he'd won twelve fights in a row and used to be called the 'Wapping Wonder'.

I was absolutely fascinated at the thought that this elderly man – this one-time 'Wapping Wonder' – was interested enough in me to tell me his life history. I began to think that there must be more in me than I knew about.

But afterwards the bus conductor, Perce, deflated my ego. When Bert went to that place reserved exclusively to men he said, 'Don't take a bit of notice of what he says because he tells everybody that old tale. I've heard it hundreds of times. He couldn't knock the skin off a rice pudding. All he ever talks about is bladders and boxing.'

Then Perce asked me why I wanted to go to Hyde Park. So I said, 'I just want to look at it.' 'No,' he said, 'you must have a reason.' 'Well,' I said, 'when you live down where I do you read about Hyde Park. Surely it's one of the sights of London, isn't it?' 'Well, I've never bothered to go there,' he said, 'and I live here.' 'Yes,' I said, 'it's just like the seaside. The residents never bother to go down on the beach and sit on the stones – it's only the trippers and visitors that do that.' 'Well,' he said, 'don't go into Hyde Park of a night on your own, it's full of prostitutes.' 'Oh,' I said, 'is it?' And far from damping my ardour I thought that was marvellous – I wanted to have a good look at them.

I'd visualized them as very alluring types of women, mysterious-looking – rather like Pola Negri the vamp who was all the rage on the films at that time. So I thought I must go and see them. 'Yes,' says Perce. 'Dressed up in all their finery on the broadwalk there. And woe betide if anyone tries to get on their pitch.' 'Well, what do they look like?' I said. 'Oh, they dress in muslins and things like that.' 'Oh,' I said, 'like Greek soldiers that wear those kind of ballet skirts.' Then Perce said, 'They might look like that but I wouldn't want to get in a fight with them. My father was in Greece during the war and he was always telling us tales about the Greek soldiers, how tough and virile they are. "Yes," he used to say, "it's more than starch that keeps those ballet skirts up."'

The implication was lost on me but everybody roared so I laughed too. After all he was providing me with refreshments even if they weren't light refreshments. Anyway I wanted a free ride back and I got one. I went upstairs again and this Perce kept running up and chatting to me and then he made a date to meet me on my next night off.

So there on my first time out in London after months and months without a boyfriend in my own home town I'd met one and made a date with him.

Mind you, until Perce had told me what a line-shooter Bert the driver was I'd found little to choose between them. In spite of his age and appearance I'd rather fancied myself going out as the girlfriend of the Wapping Wonder. But I never could abide line-shooters. I'd had a belly-full listening to George when I was kitchenmaid at my first place in Brighton.

2

GEORGE WAS THE chauffeur-gardener at the place where I first went into service in Hove and he was somewhat of a character. He hadn't always been in domestic service, which makes a difference because a man who's been in domestic service all his life — say, from the time he was fourteen — starting off as a hall boy, boot boy, page boy, or what have you and working his way up to under-footman and butler — is quite a different person from a man who's done different work and then comes into domestic service later.

Men who've been in service all their life — I wouldn't like to say they were effeminate — but they have a much quieter, gentler way of talking and they're nicer in their appearance and the way they do things. And I'm not using the word nice as a compliment here.

This George, he'd spent years in Australia which in those days was probably a far rougher country than it is now. And not only that, he'd been in the Outback, on a sheep farm. Later he was in Sydney but most of the time he was on this sheep farm, and he was always talking about the life out there. How it wasn't riddled with class distinction, how out there Jack was as good as his master. None of this 'yes sir, no sir, very good sir' and 'bloody hell how are you today sir' and bloody kow-towing just to earn a living.

Sometimes Mr Wade the butler would say, 'Well, why do you do it? If you don't like it why don't you leave and do something else?' But George was getting on and it wasn't easy to get a job in those days. George ignored him anyway. 'I tell you,' he said, 'my boss on the sheep farm, he could have bought this bloody Rev' (meaning the Reverend who we worked for) 'he could have bought this bloody Rev up ten times over, and yet at mealtimes we all sat down at the same table – boss and workers on the farm – and the boss's wife and daughter waited on us and brought us our food round and everything. Can you imagine that kind of thing going on here?'

Of course you couldn't. But it was only money that made the boss different from George and the other men on the sheep farm. And working in the Outback I shouldn't have thought that there were any grades of service. They were just workers, even the boss himself.

Maybe they had a nice home. According to George it was the last word in luxury but I can't see that it could have all the refinements that you got here. The nearest neighbour was about fifty miles away so they had to make their own life. There couldn't have been dinner parties, balls, operas and the kind of things that the well-to-do had over here. So obviously they did all mix together because otherwise it would be the boss and his wife isolated from everybody.

But you couldn't make George see that. He said we were all riddled with bloody class here. He's like a lot of people who've lived abroad and come back. The places they've left are always better. Everywhere's marvellous where they're not.

Between George and Mr Wade, the butler, there was always a sort of a feud going on. I think it was partly jealousy because being the only two men in the house they vied for attention from the servants.

Mr Wade used to think that George's manner and his speech were crude and vulgar while George thought that Mr Wade with his soft voice and his lily-white hands was no sort of a man at all. He used to say, 'Fancy having to bath and dress that old bugger upstairs. What kind of job is that for a man?'

I'd defend Mr Wade. 'Well, you drive him around don't you?' 'Oh,' he said, 'that's different.' 'And I've seen you tuck him in the back like you were tucking up a baby.' I couldn't say too much as I was only a kitchenmaid.

Then he'd say, 'Wade's no kind of a man at all. No wonder he never got married. He probably could never have performed if he had.'

I wasn't really sure what performed meant, but everybody laughed so I presumed it was something a bit on the obscene side.

George's idea of being a man was to swear and spit and intersperse words with 'bloody this' and 'bloody that' and make dirty jokes out of anything. And between him and Mr Wade there was a gulf that could never be crossed.

After one of these 'I love Australia' conversations Mr Wade asked George in a very lofty tone of voice why, if he liked Australia so much, did he ever leave it? George then gave us some long yarn about that he never would have left it but that the boss's daughter fell in love with him and as he didn't want to settle down at that time he thought he'd better leave and so he went to Sydney.

Of course the truth of the matter probably was that he started pestering the boss's daughter and the boss didn't like it, because no matter how democratic the boss was, if he was as wealthy as George made out he was, I daresay he had other ideas for his daughter than that she should marry one of his sheep men.

But anyway that was George's story. So he lit out for Sydney. Then he went off delirious about Sydney and what a marvellous place it was. He said, 'That's the place for men. They keep women in their place in Sydney. None of this bloody taking them out to the pub with you like they do over here. There aren't any pubs where bloody women can go.' And that suited George down to the ground.

'Mind you,' he said, 'the pubs are only open till six o'clock in the evening so you all knock off work at five and you make a bee-line for the pub. You swill all you can, and then you stagger home or if you can't get home you stagger to the gutter and you lie down there.' George thought it was a marvellous life.

Then he told us that while he was in Sydney he married

a widow about ten years older than he was and that her late husband had left her a lot of money. And I'm not even guessing when I say that he married her for her money. Then he persuaded her to come back to England with him.

Now he hadn't got a picture of this wife of his – we never did know her name. In fact he said very little about her. He used to go off at great length about the other women he could have married out in Australia; when he did speak about her he never had a kind word to say for her except that the only good thing she ever did in the world was to leave it.

He'd say, 'She was such a cold-hearted old bitch. She used to dole out her favours as though they were diamonds.' And he'd add, 'She was no bloody good in bed anyway and before she'd let me in with her I always had to wash and shave and clean my teeth. And what the hell's that got to do with * * * * * * *.' I use asterisks to denote my meaning because people make such a fuss about that word as though it was a new sort of vice, but the word and the deed were in use when I was young, I can assure you. In fact I never heard it called anything else.

Then he went on, 'And she made me do all the bloody work in bed. Wore me out she did.' So cook said, 'Is it still worn out, George?' She could say things like that, you see. She had a nerve. So he said, 'Oh no, I reckon I could bring it up to scratch if the occasion arose.'

Then Mr Wade said, 'I shouldn't think the occasion will ever arise.' George got so furious over this that he said, 'I'm still a man, you know. I bet if it were a contest I could beat you any day of the week.' And an argument started. But neither of them was given the opportunity to prove it. This was the vain kind of boasting you get from men.

The real reason why George used to get so livid about his wife was because when she died instead of him getting the money – the money he'd married her for – it went to her two grown-up sons. It was in trust for them and he never got a penny. So for the most part of the time George had a grieving hatred of his wife.

But once a month on his weekend off he used to go on a real bender. He'd go to the local pub and he'd order a half-pint of cider to be served in a pint glass and into this he used to tip two double whiskies and two white ports. And this was his starter. Then he would steadily drink white ports for the whole weekend.

He'd come back in on the Sunday night reeling about, and he would get maudlin.

All drinkers vary. Some people get very merry. I do. It's always worth anybody's while to buy me alcohol because they get good value for their money. I get livelier and livelier. My husband gets very quiet. Others get aggressive, which is no good at all. But old George used to get maudlin.

He'd come in, walking on the balls of his feet to keep his balance, and the tears would be streaming down his cheeks. And then he'd start a long monologue about his dear departed wife. He'd say, 'Oh, she was a lovely woman, a lovely woman. I should never have persuaded her to come back to this bloody country. She would still have been alive now if we'd stayed in Australia. This bloody country is enough to kill anybody. Do you know when she was ill I looked after her like a mother. I waited on her hand and foot. And I could have saved her if they hadn't carted her off to hospital. They killed her. They killed her in that bloody hospital. All of them bloody bed baths – that's what did it. Removing the natural juices that covered her body. Bloody water.

'But,' he said, 'I tried to save her. That last few days before she died when they had the screens around her I used to go up with a bottle of whisky. And when the nurses weren't looking I'd pull back the covers and rub her all over with it. To try and put back some of the warmth that bloody water had taken away.

'Yes,' he said, 'I worshipped every hair on that woman's body.'

Then he'd burst out crying and he'd sob himself to sleep while we tiptoed upstairs wondering how many hairs she had and how much worship George would have to have done on them.

3

GEORGE MAY HAVE loved Australia, but it wasn't until many years later that I finally went abroad myself, with my husband Albert.

The day that I heard we'd won fifty pounds on the football pools I thought that the millennium had arrived. We'd never seen fifty pounds in our lives before nor even anything like that amount.

Well, of course, straight away we started talking about what we were going to do with it. When you suddenly realize you've got fifty pounds and the largest sum you've ever had before is about ten pounds then you think that it's going to do a wonderful lot of things. First of all we thought we'd refurnish the house. We settled on things that would have come to five hundred pounds at least.

Then I said, 'Oh, I don't know. I like the place as it is.'

Then we decided we'd all have new clothes and then that idea faded out.

And then I said, 'We haven't had a holiday in years. Let's have a holiday with it.'

A holiday to me and my husband meant going somewhere in England. So we started to consider places. We didn't want to go to another seaside place, living as we did at Hove. And we didn't want to go to the country because I can't bear the country.

I don't like all those static things – the trees and fields and I don't really like animals. I wouldn't walk through a field if there was even one cow in it, never mind a herd. Have you ever noticed the way cows look at you – as if they can see right through and they don't like what they see? Scornful-like. And then they start ambling towards you. They might be going to be friendly but it's a bit too late if they get right up and you find they're not, isn't it? I don't dislike pigs, but with these factory farms it's not like the days when farmers used to let you walk around and scratch the pigs. Nowadays farming's done on such a big scale that they don't want strangers walking around.

There there are the country pubs. Everyone makes such a thing about country pubs. When you go into one every face looks up at you and you get a vista of blank faces turning towards you. They know you're a stranger to the place and they want to keep you feeling that way. You walk to the bar thinking you're a kind of leper.

The country's very nice if you like being next to nature but I hate nature.

Some people say what interesting faces country people

have got; what thinkers they must be. But I know what they're thinking. You've only got to look at the expression on their faces to know what they're thinking – bugger all. Or nothing worth thinking about, like the crops, the farm and is it going to rain and looking up at the sky and musing about it. Of course it's going to rain. It always does in the country. At any rate it does when I'm there. And another thing they're thinking is – what the devil are you doing down there? What are you after? Thoroughly suspicious they are. And even if I don't know what they're thinking I don't want to know. I don't go for a holiday to sit and wonder what people are thinking. I go to enjoy myself.

The alternative was to go to a big town like Bristol, London, or Edinburgh.

I like big towns because you're anonymous there. I like to be anonymous. I don't want the spotlight on me. Well, I didn't then; I don't mind it so much now. In any case I hadn't got many clothes to wear and not much money so I wanted to be anonymous.

I like to be in a crowd so that nobody notices you from the rest. I feel at home in a crowd and I feel at home amongst all the things that are made by man. I like everything that's machine made and man made. I like shops. I like cars. I like the new lighting that they've installed. I like everything that's mechanically made. I like things that have all been made with somebody's brain, by man's ingenuity, and it increases the stature of man to me – because after all's said and done we're only midgets here and we've only got a very short tenure of life on earth, so I think that anything that anyone's done to enhance life here is interesting and worthwhile. People keep saying that in spite of all these inventions people are no happier, but how can they tell? They don't know how happy people were that are dead and gone.

Anyway, while we were still wondering about what town to go to I had the marvellous idea of going abroad.

Of course Albert wasn't keen because he doesn't like changes. He likes things to go on in the same old way, and the very thought of going abroad, different food, different people and you can't speak a word of the language – and no country's like England. I could see these thoughts going round in his mind. I mean there's not another country in the world that's as good as ours.

It was the same when he joined the RAF during the war. He didn't fancy travelling all over the world. As it turned out he didn't have to. All the time he was in the Service he only saw one aeroplane – and that was on a scrap heap. He was in the RAF for four years – never got off the ground, and never got any farther than Yorkshire.

He had a marvellous job there. He used to go out and pick up matchsticks and barely did a stroke in the whole of the four years. Four years' rest it was. When they got tired of doing nothing they used to shovel the coal from one heap and put it in another heap.

But he'd heard about abroad – that it was the land of vice and the food was terrible. That they ate snails and slugs. That it was uncivilized and that the people all wore little grass skirts. He wasn't at all happy about the idea.

Anyway I sent to several travel companies for their brochures – you know the sort of things. They'd pictures of glamorous people in the most beautiful clothes and others lying about on the beaches with a lovely sun tan. It never rains in any of those brochures and there's never a word about what you do if it does.

One or two of the holidays we thought were marvellous but then we found out that they wanted about five hundred pounds for those. There really wasn't a lot of choice. We only had the fifty pounds from the pools though we thought we might scrape up another ten pounds – that was as much as we could do in the time available to us. So after we'd got through the brochures about three times we finally settled on a holiday that was twenty-four pounds each for ten days.

For that we would have five days in a place on the very tip of Holland so that we could make trips into Germany and Luxembourg and Belgium and we would have four days in Paris. This sounded a good bargain so we paid the deposit and then we tried to save up as much as we could.

We didn't go out anywhere. We became practically teetotallers. Believe me I wouldn't want a holiday every year if you'd got to be a teetotaller to have it. A lot of people do that. They save up their money so that they can have one big fling. I daresay we could have had a much better holiday that way, but just imagine being miserable for fifty weeks so that you can have two weeks' holiday. Then perhaps it rains all the time or the holiday doesn't go, like jelly that never sets.

In any case I think that if you've had a miserable fifty

weeks you've probably lost the capacity to enjoy yourself. But we didn't mind too much because we'd got this lump sum and we felt it wasn't too long to wait and that we were going to do something entirely different.

We felt really adventurous. Talk about Captain Cook and his voyage round the world or Christopher Columbus discovering America – the thought of Mr and Mrs Powell going abroad knocked them into a cocked hat. We were quite the big noises in our neighbourhood.

On the great day we had to be at Liverpool Street Station at eight o'clock in the morning. This meant we had to put up for the night in London and that was nearly disastrous. It cost three pounds ten for the two of us. We thought it was ruinous – absolute robbery. We had to do it because we couldn't get to Liverpool Street at eight o'clock otherwise.

We got there about quarter past seven – all eager and agog. We had a terrible job finding our party. We thought our party would be the only party. We didn't realize that we were a very small cog in a large wheel and that there were lots of other parties – much bigger parties – parties going on things with names like The Hook Continental. We didn't do anything like that. We had just an ordinary old train down to Harwich.

Finally we found our party and we got on the train. And then we met the courier. Oh, what a charming man that courier was! Of course we didn't realize then that charm was his stock-in-trade, that it was a façade and there was nothing behind it, just all charm.

He spoke to us individually and held my hand. He was a

very handsome man – I felt quite thrilled. I felt more thrilled too because incidentally the others were rather elderly – I think I was about the youngest, or looked the youngest anyway. And I was certainly the liveliest. And he sat down and held my hand. (It was a long time since any man had held my hand apart from my husband and that was old hat.) He gazed into my eyes and I felt he really cared about me. I didn't intend to throw my cap over the windmill or anything – not that the opportunity ever arose. He told us various funny little anecdotes about other trips he'd been on and things like that. You know how charming people can talk. If you try to analyse it it's all so light that it just goes away in a puff of smoke but when they're telling it to you it seems so interesting. And he was good-looking, too, which made all the difference because after all if he'd had a face like the back of a bus charm wouldn't have got him anywhere. But with charm and good looks and that lovely public-school accent . . .

Now there's a swindle for you – that public-school accent that takes you in to start with. It gets you anywhere – if you haven't got two pennies to rub together that public-school accent sees you through.

As he moved from table to table on the train everybody was saying, 'Oh, isn't he a charming man!' We were properly taken in by him.

Then he told us not to buy anything on the Continent without telling him.

'You're bound to want to bring back a piece of jewellery or some perfume,' he said. 'If you want anything just let me know and I'll tell you the shops to go to and mention my name and you'll get it cheaper.'

We swallowed this because you think, what would he tell you it for if it wasn't true? We found out later.

We eventually reached Harwich and got on the boat to go across to the Hook of Holland. The sea was rough and it was a terrible boat. There was nowhere to sit and you couldn't even get a place to hang over the side and be sick. At last I found somewhere and just lay there hoping to die.

Albert was fine – never turned a hair. And what particularly grieved me was him coming back from the bar saying, 'Do you know how much whiskies cost in there? About a third of what we pay at home and it's a bigger measure.'

What a time to choose to say a thing like that when I was calling for the angel of death. I felt so ill and every time I went to the lavatory to be sick they'd just let me be sick and then turfed me out again.

It was a horrible boat – not enough room, no chairs, no nothing. Mind you, even if it had been comfortable I couldn't have enjoyed it.

The funny thing was when we eventually got to the Hook of Holland I felt as right as rain again. It amazed me that Albert wasn't disturbed at all because he wasn't any more used to it than I was. He said it was because he's got a placid disposition that it didn't upset him, that because I'm always so eager and excited and never keep calm it happened to me.

Anyway when we arrived at the port there was a coach

waiting to take us across to this place on the very other side of Holland where we were staying – Walkenberg.

About halfway across we stopped at a place where our courier had an arrangement – where we could get coffee and cakes cheaper. So we all piled out of the coach like a flock of sheep with him at the head of us. We must have looked a very motley collection buffeted by the storm at sea. And most of us were elderly, what I call good elderly people. You could tell that never in their lives had they deviated from the straight and narrow. In we went and Albert and I had two cakes and a cup of coffee each – and we paid in francs.

I couldn't work it out there and then but when we got back in that coach I did and I said to Albert, 'Do you know what that cost us for two cups of coffee and four cakes? It cost us twelve and six. Good God, if that's the kind of place where he's got an arrangement I shudder to think what it's going to cost us anywhere where he hasn't.'

We got to Walkenberg and the hotel where we were going to stay at eleven o'clock that night. And the brochure had said that when we reached there a warm welcome would await us. Not only did no warm welcome await us – no kind of welcome at all awaited us. There was simply nobody there. Empty hotel.

We were stuck down one end of the dining-room and the courier plonked forms in front of us which we had to fill in and sign. We never saw the proprietors. And Albert and I weren't even in the hotel – we were in an annexe on the other side of the road. At the time we couldn't have cared less. We were so excited about being abroad we didn't mind where we slept.

But it just shows what kind of party we were with – they all went to bed. They come abroad and on the very first night there they go to bed at eleven o'clock – just because they are used to doing it. Well, we didn't.

We went and found our room and put our things in and went off down the sort of main street and found a place where people were sitting outside and we sat there drinking beer until two o'clock in the morning. Although we were so tired we had to prop our eyes open, we were determined to be able to say that we were drinking beer there at two o'clock in the morning. Fancy the others going to bed. Aren't the English people terrible? They've got no daring in them.

All right the beer was horrible stuff like – well, it's like water compared with English beer. I agree they've got wines that we haven't got and it's cheaper but their beer's no good at all. And Albert's a beer drinker. During the course of our holiday he got so fed up with not having a decent beer that he asked for a Guinness. He only did it once. They charged him eight and six for a glass of Guinness. They said they had to import it. No wonder nobody ever gets drunk over there because although the places are open all day you could drink that beer till you floated in it and it wouldn't do anything for you.

Still we made out we were living it up. We wrote back most glowing accounts of sitting outside this place drinking beer at two o'clock in the morning. We were frozen to death. It was cold and the beer was weak but we didn't write about that.

That was our first night there.

The idea of course of staying at this place at the very tip of Holland was to make coach trips into Germany, Luxembourg, and Belgium. And that was another stupid thing in the brochure. You had to write and say just where you'd like to sit in the coach. I chose two numbers in the middle. Well, when the coach arrived at the hotel it was already half filled with people from another tour and they weren't going to shift for us. We just had to sit where we could. And didn't some of the others moan. Albert and I didn't because we didn't really care that much. It was only a small thing.

This first day we went into Germany and the brochure said, 'Germany with its lovely castles and a trip down the Rhine – a visit to the Drachenfels and Cologne with its wonderful cathedral.' And we had a packed lunch. Oh, those packed lunches! Salami sausage, strong salami-sausage sandwiches and an orange – and we got the same every day. I couldn't eat the salami and I couldn't even eat the bread because it was so tainted with garlic.

So off we set on our coach ride and the first stop was what they called the Drachenfels. It's seven hills in a row supposed to look like a dragon. Well honestly you'd have to be as blind as a bat to ever think it looked anything like a dragon. It didn't compare with our South Downs. Just seven little lumps. The top one was very high admittedly but I couldn't see a dragon anywhere. When we got there there was a little railway that ran up to the top of this highest lump and the courier said we were all going to go up in it.

So I said, 'I'm not.'

Now on these tours they can't bear you to deviate. It worries the couriers. You've got to be the same as everybody else. By the look on his face I could see that I worried our courier.

'Oh, I couldn't go up there – absolutely impossible – it's too high,' I said.

'Oh,' he said, 'it doesn't leave the ground.'

'I hope not,' I said, 'for other people's sakes.'

He said, 'The views up there are marvellous.'

I said, 'They wouldn't be any good to me, I couldn't look at them.'

I simply refused to go. He didn't like it but he had to put up with it in the end.

So Albert and I wandered through the town on our own. And I think that was the best part of the holiday. We found a lovely little German beer garden where there was a man playing one of these xylophone things with hammers and we hadn't been there above ten minutes when he started playing English tunes. And there was dancing. It was very lively.

In the interval this man that was playing came over to us and said, 'You're English, aren't you?'

Of course we lapped this up. It gave us a feeling of prestige. So we ordered him a drink and he joined us.

He said, 'You know I can tell almost anybody's nationality now. I've been playing in this beer garden for the last twenty years.'

So I asked, 'How is it you speak English so well?'

And he said, 'Oh, I was a prisoner of war in England.'

This was in the 1914–18 War.

He chatted with us a bit. When he left I said to Albert, 'What a charming man.'

'Yes, charming thirst, too,' said Albert. 'Do you know he ordered four beers while he was sitting here and all on us.'

We were certainly paying for our experiences. Still I expect he felt we owed him something, he having been a prisoner of war.

Eventually we went back and joined the coach. Then we drove to Cologne. By the time we got there, with what I'd drunk in the beer garden I was only thinking of one thing and that was the loo.

There we were in Cologne. There was that lovely cathedral and there was the ladies' lavatory not far from it. And there were dozens of coaches – all queuing for the loo. It took me twenty minutes to get in and out and we were only allowed half an hour in the city. Talk about see Naples and die. I tore into the cathedral, looked at some gold plate and tore out again. That was Cologne for me apart from the loo.

Then we came to the Rhine. Well, the brochure had said a trip down the Rhine. We just went across in the ferry. That was our trip down the Rhine. As we went across we could see one or two castles – but what a swindle.

A mortifying thing about going in and out of these various countries was that the customs men come in and collect your passport. Yon know what passport photos are like – mine was absolutely hideous. It made me look an ugly ninety. Yet they look at it, look at you and then hand it back, so you're forced to the conclusion that it really looks like you. Very mortifying.

Anyway we got back about ten o'clock, had a hot meal which was good and Albert and I went out on the town again.

The next day was another one of these coach trips. You've got to be in the very best of health when you go on a holiday like ours because they're absolute endurance tests. We went to Luxembourg which they had said was a charming little country. I admit it was very pretty. I enjoyed it there until the courier had the idea of taking us down into a grotto.

I don't know if you've ever been in one of these underground grottoes – shocking things they are. You go down to the bowels of the earth on an iron spiral staircase and the last bit of it is slippery and slimy. I fell the last four steps into the mud at the bottom. It's dark down there and there's an underground river. You get taken in a boat on this river but you can't see a thing. And I was worried about my clothes, wondering how muddy I was, which I couldn't see down there. I think grottoes are very much over-rated things and it stank to high heaven. Well, you can imagine it, can't you? I mean it's been there since time immemorial. Everybody says 'Oo' and 'Ah' – I've never seen anything so daft. I mean you might as well put the light out and sit in your own room. At least you could sit in comfort, couldn't you?

The next day we went into Belgium which wasn't

interesting at all because they took us to Brussels, and I didn't think much of Brussels. It seemed such a dirty town to me. Apart from that there was nothing special about it at all.

Then we had one day at leisure in Walkenberg – getting our strength up as it were for the trip to Paris. This we were both looking forward to. The very name Paris conjures up images and does things for you.

The hotel we stayed in there was a good one. Mind you there was trouble from some of the party who didn't like being on the top floor. I almost felt sorry for the courier when he said to me, 'You know, it doesn't matter what party you go with, you always get people who moan and groan the entire time. You'd think that they were on a luxury tour the way they go on.' Though incidentally I noticed that at mealtimes the courier always sat at a separate table on his own and he never had the same kind of food as we did. He did far better. He was on a luxury tour by comparison.

The next day we went out shopping in the morning. Albert was going to buy me some perfume – something he'd never bought me in his life – and he asked the courier whether he had an arrangement. He had – and he directed us. Albert bought me a little tiny bottle of scent. Two guineas it cost. And when we got back to England I found we could have bought it here for forty-five shillings. Three bob we saved – on the carriage I suppose. I don't see where the arrangement came in. Let's face it, the only thing was, never in this world would Albert ordinarily have spent two guineas on perfume for me. So at least I got it, and it was marvellous. I used to use it very sparingly, a spot at a time. I hadn't used half the bottle before the scent went out of it. It doesn't always pay to be too careful.

Of course we wanted to go to a nightclub. Some people that I was doing for at home had said that we should go to the *Folies Bergère*.

'Don't pay for a seat,' they said, 'you can stand at the back for the equivalent of ten shillings and it's just as good because not only are you near the bar but you can see everything that's going on.'

So I told this to the courier.

'Oh, no,' he said 'you'll never get in the *Folies Bergère*, you have to book months ahead to get in there.'

We should really have gone and found out for ourselves, but we didn't. We thought, he must know doing these trips every year.

Then this courier said, 'I've got a better idea. I've got an arrangement with a nightclub called Eve' (and the way he said Eve made it sound ever so salacious) 'and for two pounds ten each you can sit at a proper table and share a bottle of champagne between four of you.'

We hesitated. Five pounds for two of us seemed an awful lot of money. But then to go to Paris and not be able to say you've been to a nightclub? After all, to us they seemed the main feature of Paris life. So I said, 'Oh let's do it. That'll be our last big expenditure. Let's go.'

Albert was keener than I was. Naturally it would be more interesting for a man than a woman. I couldn't see what there was going to be in it for me. If there were any turns on I wouldn't understand the language. But Albert wanted to go back and say that he'd seen a bit of nudity, so we decided to go and we gave the courier our money. When I look back and think of the money that man made I could pass out. I must admit we had taxis there – though we had to make our own way back. I'm certain he wanted to make sure we got there.

When we got inside the place it was so small. There were only two rows of tables and a bar at the back, but by the time we'd paid two pounds ten each we couldn't afford to buy any more drink anyway. Four of us sat at a table with a tepid bottle of champagne in the middle. I'd had champagne when I was in domestic service and I knew what it should taste like. This stuff was absolute rubbish. We sat there sipping it and then the first turn, if you could call it a turn, came on.

It was twelve girls nude from the waist up with very fancy dresses below the waist. There were gasps from most of the men. One man belonging to our party went as red as a beetroot. Albert sat there all nonchalant looking as though he saw such things every day. He didn't. You've never seen such a collection in all your life. Talk about twelve raving beauties – they must have gone out on the highways and byways and scoured the lot in. They were short and fat and tall and thin. And the shapes of them! Some had appendages that looked like deflated balloons – others had got them about the size of footballs which looked as though they'd blown them up before they came on the stage. Some had got such a little that you couldn't tell what sex they were; they might have been men for all we knew. And they didn't do a thing – they just kept walking round and round. There was a notice up saying 'Do Not Touch The Girls'. Even Albert said, 'Good God I'd have died before I would have touched one of them with a barge-pole.' If I tell you that Albert was bored to tears in less than five minutes you can understand what they were like.

Then came a sort of quick-patter act. Some people laughed – presumably they were French and understood what was being said. We didn't understand a word.

Then the girls came on again with different dresses from the waist down – paraded round again with their inane giggles. I said to Albert, 'Have you ever seen the female sex looking like that?' He said he hadn't and I believed him. Of course it was nothing to me – it was like bread and bread. I spent the time studying those who had pimples and where they had them.

We were there an hour. Just turns interspersed with these girls. It was dreadful. When we got up and went we left by the back stairs and as we passed a paybox I saw that we could have gone in and stood for the equivalent of twelve and six. When I told all the others they were furious and they ostracized the courier for the rest of the trip. We didn't. We wrote it down to experience. We put ourselves in his position. If we were taking a pack of greenhorns around we'd have had to have had very good characters not to have made a bit out of them.

Anyway apart from that we enjoyed Paris hugely. We

saw the Louvre, the Palace of Versailles, all those kind of places – and Paris is a beautiful and interesting city. We'd wander around on our own then sit outside the cafés watching life go by.

Twice at our hotel they served us with something like meatballs, tasty but mysterious. I was intrigued with them. And I've always been a bit pushing. I'd read in the papers about Lady So and So or the Duchess of Something or Other being abroad and coming back with the most marvellous recipes. They'd been down to the kitchen and the chef had given them these recipes which they printed.

So I said to Albert, 'I've a good mind to ask for the recipe of these meatballs.'

He said, 'I wouldn't bother. I don't want any of them when we get back home.'

'Well,' I said, 'neither do I but I just want to go back with some sort of recipe.'

So I said to the waiter – he spoke perfect English – 'Will you please ask the chef for the recipe for me?' in a nice sort of way. I thought that he might even invite me down in the kitchen.

The next day I inquired of him, 'Did you ask the chef how these meatballs are made?'

He said, 'Yes, I did, and the chef said, "God knows, I don't."'

I expect they were like those resurrection pies that the cook used to make us sometimes when I was in service. All the bits of meat that you thought had long departed this life would appear again with a pastry crust on and we used to call it resurrection pie. But did I feel deflated by that waiter. Talk about *entente cordiale*.

On the way back home we were booked to have lunch at Antwerp at a luxury hotel. And it was a luxurious place, not a bit like the hotels we'd stayed in.

We arrived at Antwerp an hour before lunch and we wandered around the town; we were then to meet in this hotel. As we went up the steps we felt like the poor relations, we'd hardly any money left by that time. It was a huge palatial entrance with a grand staircase all thickly carpeted. I was dying to go to the lavatory and I said to Albert, 'I wonder where it is?'

He said, 'Ask somebody.'

It was the sort of place where you imagined the people that went there didn't go to the lavatory.

And I said, 'Oh, I haven't got the nerve to.'

Eventually I discovered it was downstairs. You've never seen such toilets. I suppose all posh hotels are like it. It was lovely there. You didn't have to put money in and there was a whole row of basins, gold-plated taps and a separate towel at each basin. So I washed my hands. And then from nowhere sprang an old harridan holding a plate and I looked at this plate and there was nothing less than the equivalent of half a crown in it. Of course I hadn't the nerve to give her less. I should have stuck it out but she looked so intimidating.

The general run of toilets in France are something too terrible for words. They may be better now – since de Gaulle, I mean. But I'd never seen anything like the sanitary arrangements. Those awful ones they have in the street where the men's legs show below and their head and shoulders above, and you can visualize what the middle's doing. I think they're revolting.

We were on a tram once and I could see a man sort of leaning on his elbow in one of them – for all the world as though he was there to have a rest. And we went in a café on our own the first day and when I went to the toilet I stood outside waiting and a man came out. Embarrassed? I went the colour of a beetroot. Then another one I went into was just two toilets and a sort of half-tiled wall and I discovered there were three men sitting with their backs to me. They've got no reticence at all. Talk about all friends together. The funny thing is that after you've been there a couple of days – you keep drinking that awful beer that runs through you – you don't take a bit of notice. It just shows what a thin veneer civilization has really.

After lunch at this posh hotel we set off for home. The trip back wasn't too bad. It was smooth. But I still couldn't enjoy a cheap whisky because after we'd bought some cigarettes and some wine to take back, we'd nothing left. By the time we got to Liverpool Street Station we were a sorry-looking lot.

In the brochure there was something about the friends we were going to make and I'd had visions of exchanging addresses and writing to these friends and keeping in touch. Instead of that – not only was nobody speaking to the courier – they weren't even speaking to each other.

When we got back home I said to Albert, 'Let's have another look at this brochure and go through the things that weren't as they said they would be.' But as we read it again we saw in very small print at the bottom 'Turn to the back page'. So we turned to the back page. There again in very small print was written 'On this tour the agents exercise the right to make any alterations that circumstances may demand'. So that it had just been that in our case the circumstances had been very demanding.

4

TO SAY THAT I was surprised to get a date after being in London barely a week is to put it mildly. I couldn't believe my good fortune. Surely, I'd thought, there must be more of a scarcity of females up in London than there is down in Hove. And not only that – I'd got a date with a man who had a regular job. A bus conductor.

My mother was always on to me about the merits of getting a young man who had a regular job. 'It doesn't matter how small the wages are,' she said, 'so long as it comes along regularly every Saturday.' My poor old mum must have felt it with Dad's irregular work. Some weeks there was no money at all. She often used to say to me, 'If only I could be sure of two pounds a week I'd be in heaven.' So there was I, in heaven, too.

As I've explained, my afternoon and evening out was on Wednesday, except of course if they happened to have a dinner party on that night. If they had, you were expected to give it up. You weren't expected to have made plans so it couldn't matter to you whether you had Wednesday, Thursday or any other day.

Anyway this Wednesday was all right and I met my Percival. He'd told me he liked to be called Percival. I thought both Perce and Percival were terrible names, but after all beggars can't be choosers.

When I met him he told me he was going to take me to his mother's to tea. Well, if he'd told me he was taking me to the Ritz I couldn't have been more astounded. I mean in our circles you were never taken to tea to a boy's house unless you'd been going steady with him for a long time. To be taken to tea to his mother's house was tantamount to being engaged to him. This put the wind up me properly. It was going to be an ordeal meeting Perce's mum. It hadn't happened to me before. I'd never been out with a boy long enough ever to get round to that stage. But I knew girls who had and they'd told me how they'd had to run the gauntlet. They said it was something that required the strongest nerves.

Anyway to Percival's home we went to meet his mother – or 'Ma' as he called her. I'd never have dared call her Ma even if she'd become my mother-in-law, which she never did. I'd never have dared call her anything but Mrs Tait, which was her name.

She was about five feet nothing in size but in strength of character I reckon she was about ten feet tall. I was overwhelmed by her. There was no sign of a husband and at first I wondered what had happened to him – whether he'd departed this life or what. But she told me a very mysterious story how one day he went off to visit some relatives. He took nothing with him because he was only going for the day – no money and no clothes – and was never heard of again. He never came back. He never even visited the relatives. So I said to her, 'Whatever did you do, Mrs Tait – did you notify the police?' 'Oh, yes,' she said. 'But you must have nearly gone mad with worry,' I said. 'No,' she said, 'it was the Lord's will.' See, she was one of those who when anything happened it was the Lord's will. She asked me how old I was and as I'd already put two years on my age and told Perce that I was eighteen I had to tell her the same.

During the course of the tea I discovered that she'd had three sons, triplets, and she'd called them Lancelot, Tristram, and Percival which was the one I'd got – this Percival. She'd got the names out of a book called *Morte d'Arthur*, which she'd found on a second-hand bookstall when she was pregnant. At that time I'd never even heard of the book, but later when I did I found it was the last book I'd have read when I was pregnant. I never heard such rubbish. Tales of knightly chivalry when you're lugging around a stomach the size of a pumpkin. I always was large when I was pregnant and after all she was carrying triplets.

Also, I couldn't help feeling that the names Lancelot, Tristram, and Percival were unfortunate names to have to go to school with. Percival told me that they were shortened to Lance, Tris, and Perce so I suppose they got away with it. But when I was at school there was a girl in our class named Cecilia who didn't. Then we had an Anastasia and her mother said to the teacher that she didn't want her name shortened; she was to be called by the whole name. We did just that and she had a hell of a time. You know how cruel children can be. I was glad my name was ordinary. Nobody wanted to be different then – not at the kind of school I went to anyway.

After we'd had tea this Mrs Tait subjected me to such an interrogation as to my antecedents that I felt she'd missed her vocation. She should have been a member of the Spanish Inquisition. It was so ridiculous too, as it was the very first time I'd ever been there and it was quite likely I wouldn't go again. I couldn't understand at first why Perce didn't put his oar in and tell her to shut up. Then of course I realized that he was over thirty years old and he must have got used to it. By his age he'd probably brought a number of girls home to be inspected and rejected.

I discovered that Lancelot and Tristram had escaped their mother's clutches, for which I didn't blame them. One had gone to Canada and one had gone to Australia and they'd both been gone about ten years. During this time they were writing letters home saying how much they missed their mother or so she said, but neither of them had made the trip back. So I could see by all this interrogation and all this talk that she was determined not to lose Perce and I suppose you couldn't really blame her. She'd got no husband and only that one son to keep her, so life would have been difficult for her without him. Yes, it would have had to have been a very determined girl that would stick to Perce if she'd been got at by his mother every time he took her home.

Much to my relief, at about half past six Perce suggested

that we go out. Just him and me. We were to have gone to the films but when we got outside he suggested we went to a dance instead. Well, I wasn't too keen on going to a dance. I had to be in by ten o'clock which would mean leaving about half past nine, but he said he didn't want to be late because he'd got an early shift, so off we went.

It was a small suburban hall, not a bit like the Palais de Danses that you get now. Just a large bare room with a few fancy shades hanging down and a three- or four-piece band right at the end. The floor was smothered with some kind of powder stuff. It was the kind of place where they held meetings and socials through the week, not a proper dance hall. It only cost one and three to go in and although it was still only seven o'clock there were already a lot of people there.

Most of the girls were dressed up. Some had got knee-length dresses and some had got what were fashionable at that time, dresses hanging down longer at the back than at the front. And they wore very light flesh-coloured stockings which were all the go too in those days.

The men hadn't bothered at all. They were mostly in Oxford bags – trousers about two foot wide at the bottoms. To me they seemed a very weedy-looking lot, but as I'd gone with a partner I could afford to be critical.

Of course like all dance halls at the time there were a lot more girls than boys and there were none of these courtly gestures of a boy escorting you back to your seat. No, they just left you bang in the middle of the floor and went and congregated at one end while you made your own way back to sit and become a wallflower again.

I couldn't help thinking how pretty and sophisticated the London girls looked in comparison to those from my home town. Some of them had got Eton crops which were coming into fashion at that time. My sister used to have an Eton crop but you've got to have the right face for it. With my kind of features if I'd had an Eton crop I'd have just looked like a hard-boiled egg with a top knot.

After a time Perce went off to get me a cup of coffee, and while he was gone a young man came up and asked me to dance. Well, I thought, here goes. I'm not bound to Perce. After all he hadn't bought me body and soul for one and three which was all he'd spent so far. So I got up to dance with this fellow.

'I haven't seen you here before,' he said. 'No,' I said, 'it's my first time.' 'Are you with anyone?' he said. 'Yes, I've come with a boyfriend.' He turned a bit pale at this. 'Won't he mind you dancing with me?' 'Why should he mind?' I said. 'Oh,' he said, 'that just shows you're a stranger here. When you come with a boyfriend you don't get up and dance with someone else.' I'd seen quite a few girls dancing with more than one partner and I said so. 'Ah,' he said, 'but they all know each other or else they're related. No complete stranger who comes with a boyfriend ever dances with anyone else. What will you do if he's annoyed?' I said, 'What will you do?' He swallowed hard and then said, 'I shan't do anything – I'm off. You see I'm known here.' And he left me in the middle of the floor.

Anyway just at that moment Perce came back. He'd seen what had happened and his face was black as thunder.

I felt as though I'd been caught in some sort of orgy. He said, 'Never you do that again. I'm known here and it makes me look bloody silly when I bring a girl and I leave her for a minute and she dances with somebody else.'

Now who'd have thought there was all that ridiculous protocol? All this 'I'm known here'. What a funny way of going on. I thought about my mother and how she'd said that London dance halls were dens of vice. Well, I thought, she should come and see this one. Talk about the height of respectability. And if this was London, the city of sin, it looked as if I was going to leave it as unsullied as when I came to it.

Anyway, eventually Perce calmed down. He even saw me to my bus. But I remember thinking on my way home – this isn't going to last much longer, and in short supply though men were I can't say it worried me. Still, before Perce and I parted we'd arranged another meeting for the following Wednesday – a proper glutton for punishment I was.

5

LITTLE DID I think when I'd agreed to meet Percival that Wednesday that this included his Ma once again. Apparently every Wednesday evening when he was on early shift they went together to a Meeting. I soon found out that going to a meeting meant going to a sort of church thing for an hour and that they belonged to a strict rigid religious sect called 'The Ruth Elders'. I'd never heard of it before, nor have I ever heard of it since. But according to his Ma it was a breakaway from the Evangelical Church. They'd done away with all forms of ceremony, no infant baptisms, no stained-glass windows and no ceremonial robes or anything like that.

I didn't see how I could get out of going. I thought perhaps it was another test to see if I would be a fit companion to go out with her son. I mean, I'd already had the interrogation about my antecedents the first time and I thought – oh well, this is the second round.

Mind you, I'd already made up my mind that nothing on

earth would induce me to see his Ma again because I knew that it was becoming a sort of tug-of-war and I wasn't going to join battle. If he wanted his Ma more than he wanted me well then that was that as far as I was concerned. I didn't really care.

So we went to this hall where The Ruth Elders met and most decidedly she never exaggerated when she said that they went in for stark simplicity.

It was just a bare hall – cold as charity, wooden floors with hard wooden benches and lit by a gas light. There were about thirty people there and much to my relief we sat down in the back row.

Everyone was old. Apart from me Perce was the youngest by far. They had a pastor though I don't know if you would call him a pastor. I call him a pastor for want of a better word, but he didn't wear any dog collar or cassock and surplice or anything like that at all. He was just dressed in a dark suit.

He said a little prayer to start with and we all had to kneel down on this wooden floor. I was thinking about my silk stockings all the time. Then he gave about a ten-minute sermon promising us that hell and damnation would follow for anybody who deviated from the straight and narrow path. I remember looking around at the congregation and thinking that such a chance would be a damned fine thing for any of them.

After the sermon there was silence for about a couple of minutes and then all of a sudden to my amazement, and to my horror too, some woman got up and started declaiming loudly about the sins that she'd committed since she'd been there last.

Talk about audience participation. One after another they all got up and started shrieking out in a loud voice of all their wickednesses. And these sins were the silliest things. Like they'd taken too much pride in their appearance or they had a ha'penny too much given them in change and they hadn't gone back to the shop with it. And one of them had lost her temper at home. The last female that stood up – she got into such a frenzy, I thought she was going to throw a fit.

Looking back on it I suppose all this bursting forth was a kind of outlet for their repressed sexual emotions which no doubt they never gave rein to at home or elsewhere.

There she was ranting and raving and thrusting her arms towards the pastor. I said to myself – steady, girl, here it comes: the big sin of the week. Then came the awful truth. One morning she felt so tired she didn't get up and make her husband's breakfast. Well, I ask you. Omission it might be – sin never. It was all so piddling.

Then, after calling for a few minutes' more silence, the pastor said that if there were any troubled souls there, would they come up to him for advice, and he'd lay his hands on them.

Well search me, if I'd had all the troubles in the world nothing would have induced me to have gone up and let him lay his hands on me. I mean, all right if he'd been one of those intense, spiritual-looking aesthetic priests, but a portly, smug-faced man that looked as if he'd just left the mayoral banquet – nothing would have induced me to have gone up there. In any case they'd have all passed out if I'd have told them my sins, and even mine weren't that bad. That was the end of The Ruth Elders.

Then Perce said, would I like to go round to the working men's club with him? I'd never been to a working men's club before and I had no idea what it was like so I agreed. This was going to be another first and last for me.

Oh, what dumps they are! Maybe they're not now but they were then. It was another bare room with nothing in it at all. No carpet, no rugs, no nice tables. Talk about a boost to the male ego. Everything was there for men but nothing for females at all. Men had got billiard tables, card tables, and darts but all the women did was just stick up at one end of the room. It was a working men's club but never mind about the working men's wives or their girlfriends.

When we got there Perce dumped me at the women's end while he went off to play billiards. This after the prayer meeting was not my idea of going out with a young man.

Yet none of the other women seemed to mind about being down there, with their boyfriends and husbands up the other end all clubbing together. Some were knitting and some were just talking. They tried to be friendly, I've got to give them their due. They asked me what I did so I said I was in domestic service and they said, 'Oh, a skivvy!' Not nasty at all; it was just their name for domestic servants, but you could tell by the tone they said it in that none of them would ever be seen dead in service, for which I didn't blame them.

One of them worked in a fried fish and chip shop. She needn't have bothered to tell me that because you could smell it a mile off. One of them took rather a fancy to me. She was a woman of about thirty-five – not married – a barmaid. Violet her name was. She said to me, 'I wouldn't stick that life. Why don't you take a barmaid's job?'

Why? My mum and dad would've gone stark raving mad if I'd ever written home and told them I was a barmaid. They'd have been up post haste to rescue me. All right. Nowadays barmaids have got a certain status. Pubs are nothing like the riotous places they were in the old days, and half of them have been made into these cocktail-lounge things. But then a barmaid was a low job. There weren't many of them – mostly there were barmen.

I remember when Mum and Dad used to get me to go round on a Saturday dinnertime to get half a pint of Burton from the bottle and jug department. It was right next door to the public bar and the language of the barmaid in there was worse than any bargee or labourer that I've ever heard.

This Violet, she said it was a lovely life – jolly and lively. I daresay it was, but I couldn't help thinking to myself that men don't marry barmaids. She was an example. She was thirty-five and she wasn't married and she was already beginning to go off, as you might say. Oh no, being a barmaid wasn't for me.

After I'd been there for about an hour Perce brought me over a cup of tea and then he said that they were going up to the pub for an hour to have a drink. Naturally I thought we were all going too. So I got up and he sort of hissed at me under his breath and said, 'No, not you. You stay here.'

I was infuriated at this. Stuck there with all these women while he went out to the pub. So I said, 'I'm certainly not stopping here' – hissing at him too under my breath. And he hissed, 'Do you want to make me look a bloody fool in front of all my mates?' Well, what could I do. I just had to let him go. But what an idea of enjoyment.

My mum would never let my dad go out without her and I don't blame her in the least. When you get married to a man you never want to let him go out without you because once he starts that he'll do it for ever. When a woman gets married it's her whole life – the man is her life. But to a man marriage is just another part of his life because he's still doing exactly the same sort of work that he did before he got married. And he's still got all his pals and he doesn't want to give them up. So you've got to keep a tight rein on them.

I remember when I first got married Albert, my husband, and I had always gone out together. Then I had the first baby. And when the baby was about a fortnight old Albert said, 'I think I'll go over the road and have a drink.' I said, 'Well, all right, I'll come too.' So he said, 'What about the baby?' 'It's your baby as much as mine,' I said, 'and if you can leave it so can I.' I wasn't having any of that kind of lark.

Anyway Perce and the rest of the men poured out over to the pub and of course no sooner had they gone than a sexual conversation started, and amongst these females it was too terrible for words.

The married women went into great length and detail. The act of sex might have been a private act physically but it certainly wasn't private verbally. I'd never heard such things in my life. And the jokes they were telling.

Mind you, it did make a change from The Ruth Elders. But doesn't that show you the duplicity of people? That Perce must have known the kind of things that went on in the club.

They say that women are complex creatures, but believe me you can't beat a man when he wants to put one over on you. This was one of my first lessons but I have had many others since.

After a bit this Violet got me on one side and said, 'I wouldn't waste any time on that Perce if I were you, because you'll never get him away from his mother.' She said, 'He's been coming to this club for the last eight or nine years and he often brings a girl but they never last long.'

I knew it was true that you wouldn't get him away from his mother. You couldn't really blame her because there's nothing stronger than the maternal instinct. They don't think that they're distorting their son's life – that they're making them not a real man. He had a feeling for his mother that he shouldn't have had. I don't mean to say that they had an incestuous relationship. Of course they didn't, but a man who's been living with his mother alone year after year, he'd be simply no good as a husband.

To start with you can never measure up to their mother. And then they're not the kind of men that are interested in sex because if they were they wouldn't have tied themselves to their mother in the first place. The fact is that the maternal relationship is so big that they haven't got enough left for anyone else. I mean, even if you went all out and got them it'd be more like living with your brother than a husband.

So there was Violet telling me all this, but I already knew as much myself.

She said, 'The only time that you can ever get his kind up to scratch is if you get them half canned or if you put in all the spade work yourself. In any case,' she said, 'the end result isn't worth bothering about.'

So with her advice and my own experience I decided that night was the parting of the ways for me and Perce. What with his mother fixation, his 'men only' drinking and his Ruth Elders – even if I'd ever got him to the altar, which I doubt – I'd have had a scratchy sort of married life. For people mixed up with these strict religious sects the word sex is taboo and the deed of the four-letter word is something too terrible for them to contemplate.

6

THOUGH I WASN'T impressed by the working men's clubs, I have always been a fan of pubs. You might say that I've known three generations of pubs. There's pubs I knew when I was a child, there's the pubs I knew in my early married life in London and elsewhere, and there's the pubs that exist now. And the differences are vast.

When I was a child, it was true to say that for the middle and upper classes the Englishman's home was his castle, but for the working-class man the pub was his castle. It was a place where no do-gooders had the right or the courage to come as they did to one's home where, for the sake of the charity they distributed, you had to listen to them and pretend that you believed in what they were telling you. Once you got in a pub you, metaphorically speaking, drew up the draw-bridge and there you were – lord of all you surveyed. And what you surveyed was lively, warm, and happy. It might have only been a superficial atmosphere and it could be quick to change. It often did, ending up in a free-for-all fight, but even those were enjoyable. After all that's part of a castle's life, isn't it – fighting?

When I was about seven or eight I often used to go into the pub on a Saturday dinnertime to get my mum and dad half a pint of Burton. The bottle and jug department used to be right next door to the public bar and the people who were in it were the kind of people that I saw every day of the week – people who lived round us – but you'd never have thought they were the same people. As I looked through they seemed to have changed their characters completely. The way they spoke and the way they laughed – they had come alive.

Kids used to be allowed in the bottle and jug department – it didn't matter how young you were. I think there was just some peculiar rule whereby it didn't matter about your age if you got it in a jug but you couldn't have it in a bottle with a screw top. Why – I don't know. Whether they thought you might drink it out of the bottle – but I should have thought it more likely that you'd do that with a jug. Mind you, I never drank any of my mum and dad's half-pint of Burton – if I had my life wouldn't have been worth a tinker's cuss. Dad used to measure it out – to him it was liquid gold – and if there was short measure I had to go back with it. When you could only afford half a pint you saw that you got it. Then it used to be measured out fairly between Mum and him.

The life that used to go on in the pubs was as good as a variety show. Some nights my mum and dad used to let us stand at the doors and we'd be fascinated by it all. Publicans allowed hawkers to go in selling matches, bootlaces, toys, scurrilous ditties, and a sure cure for the clap. Not that we knew what the clap was then, but it used to sell well – the cure I mean.

In our pub there used to be a man: on a Saturday night somebody would buy him a pint of beer and he used to balance it on his head while he slowly undressed as far as the waist, and if he could get everything off without spilling it he could drink it for free. And sometimes after this he'd try dressing again for another wager but it was much harder and many a time he upset it and it'd go to waste.

I know a lot of people used to think it terrible leaving kids outside a pub. But my parents were very good. They wouldn't leave us there when it was freezing cold. If they could see we were getting fed up they'd bring us biscuits or a bottle of lemonade between us. But generally we didn't worry; there was so much going on. Today I don't like to see it – but only because I reckon the kids might die with boredom.

There was another man who used to come in who said he had a performing flea. He used to call this flea Algernon and he'd hold a matchbox in his hand, then open it a bit, and say, 'Would you like to see Algernon do a somersault?' And then he'd talk to this flea and say, 'Come on, Algernon, show them how clever you are. There, did you see him do it?' And then back to the box again and he'd say, 'Would you like to see Algernon do a double somersault? Come on Algernon, alley oop.' Then he'd lose Algernon and he'd cry, 'Oh, he's lost. Algernon's lost. He's fallen in love – I think with you, miss, or you, sir.' But nobody got panicky; nobody worried about a flea loose because fleas along with flies were the thing that you had in your home. For fleas, as I've said, we used Keatings powder and for flies those terrible sticky things you hung from the ceiling. My mother used to put one up sometimes on a Saturday dinnertime and by Sunday there wouldn't be one space left – they'd be two or three deep, you know, and it was horrible if you hit it with your head. So nobody worried that Algernon was roaming. Then he'd say, 'Look lady, he's on your coat.' And he'd go to pick him off her coat and he'd lose him again. And then it would be, 'There he is on the wall.' And everybody would stand gaping, their eyes going all round the walls. But the thing was, there never was a flea – it was an imaginary Algernon. But there would be the customers following imaginary Algernon, until at last it struck the landlord what money he was losing because while they were looking they weren't buying any beer. So eventually either the customers would buy the man beer to console him for the loss of Algernon or the publican would eject him.

Another person we used to watch was an old man who stood outside holding his hand out with a ha'penny in it waiting for someone to add to it. Perhaps when someone went in they wouldn't contribute but when they came out they were feeling far more mellow so they'd cough up.

Then he'd dart into the pub – have a drink – then come out again – put his hand in his pocket for another ha'penny and start once more.

Sometimes this happy jolly atmosphere would change and instead of the sort of friendly swearing a hard note would creep in and it would be swearing in earnest – and then the fighting would start. But the publicans didn't mind. There weren't many barmaids, mainly barmen – great hefty fellows who also acted as chuckers-out. We'd stand away from the doors and out the troublemakers would come, thrown on to the pavement covered in sawdust and beer. We used to think it was marvellous – as good as going to the pictures – and free too.

Some twenty to thirty years after this, when I was married and Albert and I used to go into pubs, they were different. Or at any rate they seemed different. Most of them had three bars – public, private, and saloon – and people seemed to keep to their particular definition. The type of customer was different or dressed different. In the public bar would be the working class. Working class, that is, who never dressed up at any time, never changed and wanted the bar to be just spit and sawdust, darts and dominoes. Then in the private bar would be the kind of people who didn't want to go in the public bar where the language and the people were too strong and salty for them, but nevertheless didn't want to mix with what they thought were the snooty ones in the saloon. The saloon bar was a mixture. You'd get the working-class people who when they'd finished their work would dress themselves up and go there as well as the well-to-do who used it as a matter of course. We used to go in the private bar during the week because it was cheaper, but at a weekend we dressed ourselves up and always went in the saloon. It was a sort of class and dress consciousness.

Although they weren't the same kind of places they were still friendly and cheerful. Full of people, especially at weekends, and they'd still got the mahogany and mirrors and brass beer handles – the impedimenta of a pub. Barmaids were in the ascendancy, and to have a barmaid instead of a barman made a vast difference. They were bright, cheerful girls, often peroxided or hennaed which was all the go in those days, and with the beer or spirits they dispensed a fund of good humour. They'd listen to you; if you had a hard-luck tale, they'd be sympathetic, or if you told them a bawdy story they'd screech with laughter. They were all things to all people and they added sort of another dimension to the pub.

I don't know how they stood socially. It sounds terrible to compare them to prostitutes – they weren't of course – but just as there is a type of man who likes prostitutes and prefers them to anyone else, so there was a type of man who liked barmaids. But never in a million years would they ever have dreamt of marrying them. They loved them, called them 'sweetheart', told them things they'd never have told their wives, shared their business troubles, their office jokes, and you know how obscene office jokes are, laughed with them and teased them and often bought them presents. They treated them I suppose as a wealthy man might his kept woman, and they expected the same things from her, except of course the sex bit, but marry them – never.

Christmas in the local used to be like the old childhood Christmases. The decorations, Christmas trees and a spontaneous kind of gaiety. The landlady would come round with the gin bottle for the ladies, and the landlord would dispense free beer to the men. In the local Albert and I used in Chelsea it was a mixed kind of pub – rich and poor – but all knew each other, and although Albert and I didn't join any of the large parties it wasn't because we wouldn't have been welcome. It was just that we didn't accept from people drinks that we couldn't afford to return. And people respected that. But you could talk to anyone in there. You didn't feel ostracized because you weren't in a position to buy a round. And the talk was interesting and friendly. You could either pass the time of day or have half an hour's intelligent conversation – so that for very little money you could have an enjoyable social evening.

I suppose pubs really started to change after the last war, and that change is now almost complete. Occasionally you'll come across one of those pubs that's still got the glass, the mahogany and a whiff of the old atmosphere, but you are made to feel an alien – an unwelcome stranger. I suppose the landlord doesn't want you because the pub might become popular. Then he'd have to employ staff, the brewers would raise the rent, he'd lose the regulars he's used to and the way of life that suits him. And the customers think on the same lines. They've seen what's happened in other pubs and they don't want it to happen there – and who's to blame them.

I think that television was the beginning of the end of pubs as we knew them, as television has been the death of so many things. I remember when it first came in how the pubs tried installing television in the bar. That was an absolute disaster. If you've ever been into a pub in the early days of television you'd know what I mean. The bar would be full of people all watching. And apart from the noise of whatever programme was on, it would be as silent as the tomb. You'd go in and ask for your drink in a whisper. And if you didn't want to watch the thing, which we didn't, you'd start a *sotto voce* conversation. Then the heads would flash round and shh you like snakes. Oh, it made a real jolly evening out. It didn't take long for publicans to realize that installing television was no answer to this falling trade, because the people watching television spent very little money and the people that didn't want to watch were so bored that they gave up coming into the pubs. And that I think was the beginning because people lost the habit. This doesn't apply in the City and the West End of London. There, pubs are lovely places to go to, particularly at dinnertime. You get food, drink, and conversation. No, it's the provinces that seem to have given up trying.

Some people blame the decline of pubs on the influence of women. I don't agree of course. To my mind the presence of women has done away with a lot of drunkenness. Whereas men on their own didn't care how they got – the kind of disgusting condition men can get into left on their own, over-indulging in foul jokes and things like that – when they've got a woman with them or near them they've got to not only moderate their language, they've got to moderate their drinking too. Because the money's got to do for two people instead of one. No, I think women add a great deal to pubs. Surely a pub is a place for social intercourse. Well, if it's only going to be exclusively for men, they've got very little conversation, because men are inherently lazy about using their brains. They're not interested in talking about anything but their work, dirty stories, what girl they've been out with or what girl they hope to go out with, and what they're going to do to her when they get her out. Women have changed this. So I think they've done a lot for pubs.

In any case with the equality of the sexes rearing its ugly head, as men put it, why shouldn't women share in the social life? When you marry a man you don't expect that your domain is going to be just the home, do you? An example of what it used to be like is this. About eight o'clock at night the man says, 'Well, I'm off to have a drink. Cheerio. I shan't be late. Have my supper ready for me when they close.' What the devil did he think you were? He could've waited till the cows came home for his supper as far as I was concerned. And when he came back he'd have found I was out too. That's what so many working-class wives had to put up with. They were nothing but unpaid housekeepers. I wasn't and I never intended to be.

What I think has changed pubs, and what may eventually almost destroy them, is 'nationalization'. Because that is what is happening. They're being 'nationalized' by financiers.

Instead of having any number of local breweries, family concerns, owning a few pubs in a small area – we've now got four or five industrial giants run by accountants and computers from boot-box blocks of offices dictating what the public will drink. The pubs are managed for them by the faceless civil servants they now choose as landlords, tenants, or managers.

In the days of the small brewers they knew about local tastes and interests. They studied their customers. If it was thought that something was wrong with the beer the brewer would come round and find out what. I'm willing to bet that half the people who brew the stuff now have never tasted it in their lives.

And the way they decorate and furnish places! They look clinical, like something out of the Ideal Home Exhibition. But pubs aren't homes or they shouldn't be. You come out of your home for new surroundings and what do you find? Thick carpets, soft armchairs, a sort of cocktail-lounge effect. And the breweries say that's what the customers want. How do they know? Did they ask them? And if the customers want that why aren't they there to use it? A lot of people – people like my husband and me – feel out of place in these cocktail-lounge kind of places. But you've got to go there because they've done away with the private bar and you've only got two grades now – public bar and this kind of phoney set-up.

Then they haven't got the drinks you want. My husband likes drinking beer – mild beer. And they don't serve it except in the public bar. And when you ask you can see them thinking, 'What are you doing in here then if you can't afford expensive drinks?'

It's not just television. Maybe it's because in an affluent society people don't need what we do – the support and company of other people as a sort of prop in our leisure time. Perhaps money does that for you. Makes you independent. But if that's what being rich means, I don't want it. I still need to depend on people for my enjoyment.

It was strange how packed the pubs used to be during the war – and I don't think this was just because we had to have the alcohol. In a time of adversity we wanted the feeling of togetherness. It's a pity that it takes a war to give us this kind of unity with each other.

7

GLADYS WAS THE under-housemaid at my first place in London. She was a year older than me and although she wasn't what you'd call a pretty girl she had loads of personality. I used to look forward to our Sundays off together. Every other Sunday we got and we always started by going out to tea.

We used to go to rather posh places where they had all gold paint and plaster cupids and marble pillars, and for the price of a pot of tea and two or three cakes you could really feel that you were living it up. We'd sit there and there'd be well-dressed people all around us with their high-faluting talk. And wooing young men would have their girls there.

Personally I could never see why people wanted to do their courting in restaurants. I think there's nothing less conducive to love than seeing people opposite you chewing all the time. I never could understand this mania that English people have for eating out. Either the food is so wonderful when you eat out that you're not in the least bit interested in your partner, or else you're so interested in him that you aren't taking a bit of notice to what you eat.

When I was trying to get a young man I'd never go eating because the way some young men eat – shovelling away at their food, chewing with their mouths wide open – you can't help thinking, 'Heavens above, would I have to sit opposite that every day of my life if we got married?' So it's best not to know.

All men have got defects, we know that, but you don't want them paraded in front of you before you've taken them on, do you? After you're married you can do your best to eradicate the defects but you can't start eradicating before you've got your man up the aisle.

Then there's the kind of man who always props a news-paper in front of him. Of course you can't see him eating but you want a man to talk to you.

The whole art of spending a married life together is not just popping up to bed. Your husband should be able to talk to you. Perhaps when you've been married years you don't worry so much, but when you first get married you visual-ize dainty food, a nice tablecloth and the man sitting there and talking to you about interesting things. Of course it's all in your mind. It doesn't really materialize, but that's what you think it's going to be.

So I don't think eating goes with courting.

Drinking is another thing altogether. You go into a pub or a lounge and you have a glass of wine with a stem to it and you sit there holding the stem and you gaze into each other's eyes over this glass of wine. You can really feel romantic like that. Love and wine go together but love and food don't.

Mind you, you never found any young men in those kind of teashops because no unattached males ever went there. You'd find them in Lyons if you wanted to pick up a couple, but never if you went in those kind of semi-posh places.

Still we had to give up the chase some time, didn't we? We couldn't devote our whole lives to looking for men.

One particular Sunday we decided that we'd go to the Trocadero. It was a place that we'd only been in once before and we'd found it too expensive for us. It was the height of luxury. They had very deep carpets and beautiful subdued lights, and there was a band that played sweet and low music.

One of Gladys's uncles had just got a job there as a trolley waiter and we thought we might get things a bit cheaper so we decided to chance it.

It really was marvellous.

They served tea in silver-plated teapots and instead of knives to cut your cake with you got those little forks with two prongs. I know it's daft but nevertheless you feel that you're really moving with the high-ups when you don't have a knife to eat your tea with.

The only thing was that Gladys's uncle struck a somewhat incongruous note in all these luxurious surroundings. I suppose it was because he was over sixty and he'd got flat feet, a very red nose and he'd a scraggy neck so his Adam's apple bobbled up and down in a very peculiar way the whole time he talked.

Still when he brought the trolley to us I'd never seen such lovely cakes in my life – and he whispered to Gladys, 'Have two for the price of one.' And we did this two or three times.

The beauty of the Trocadero was that you didn't have to hurry. In some of the teashops we went in we didn't like to linger because somebody might be wanting the table. But in there nobody seemed to bother. It was a sort of afternoon ritual. We sat there nearly two hours.

And these teapots that they gave you. You could get four cups of tea for each of you if you kept sticking the hot water in. Of course eventually it came out almost like pouring it straight out of the hot-water jug but that didn't matter. We got four cups each so we sat there sipping away and listening to the band.

And the toilets there! They were an absolute revelation. There were three of them and they were lovely ones. The walls stretched right up to the ceiling – not like those where there's no top or bottom. There were basins to wash your hands and as many towels as you wanted.

So we really had a wonderful afternoon at the Trocadero.

That evening Gladys suggested we went round to see her aunt – the wife of this uncle. They lived just off Ladbroke Grove.

It was a terrible place. A house with five floors if you included the basement, and there were three families living on every floor. Four rooms on each floor. One family had two rooms and the other rooms had one family each. The smell when you went in the passage was appalling. It was compounded of stale food, dirt, and the smell of sweaty humanity.

Mind you, Gladys never turned a hair. It could have been the roses of Picardy for all she knew. Maybe coming from Stepney as she did she was used to it.

I've seen some slummy places in my own home town but nothing to compare with that. You didn't dare put your hand on the banister – it was coated in filth. Each particular family was supposed to take turns doing their bits of the stairs down from one floor to another, but with three families on each floor there were quarrels as to whose turn it was and nothing ever got done.

Gladys's aunt lived on the top floor. All they had in the way of water was one small sink on the landing halfway up and that had to do for those two floors. So that there were six families using one tiny sink and one lavatory.

The contrast between this and the Trocadero!

I said to Gladys, 'Surely your uncle can afford a better place than this?' She said that he probably could if he stuck a job but he drank a lot, which accounted for his red nose. Apparently he was always drinking and losing his job and I suppose that was what they were reduced to. It was a terrible hole! I didn't know how anyone had the spirit to keep clean there.

Gladys's aunt had been in domestic service and she bitterly regretted ever leaving it. She'd loved the place where she worked. And she was delighted to have an audience of two who themselves were in service. She was on about Sir and Madam and Master Gerald and Miss Sarah. I thought it was absolutely stupid. After all those years still calling the people you worked for Sir and Madam and Master and Miss. It just shows you, doesn't it – there is a type of person who likes domestic service? They feel there's a certain prestige attached to serving the high and mighty.

While I was there she got out some newspaper cuttings about this Miss Sarah who was in the suffragette movement and I was interested in this.

This Miss Sarah wasn't one of the more militant ones – not like the Pankhurst woman. She didn't go around setting fire to churches, slashing valuable paintings or putting lighted paper through people's letter boxes. But there were a couple of newspaper photos of her. In one of them she'd got a policeman's helmet stuck on her head and in the other she was there with a lot of other women debagging a policeman.

I must say I was surprised because I hadn't realized that these suffragettes came from well-to-do homes. I couldn't think that people who'd got a comfortable home and didn't have to work could really feel there was anything they ought to fight for.

My mother was a very strong-minded woman – what you would call a militant woman – but she never bothered about the rights of women. So long as she'd got the vote in her home – and, believe me, she had – she couldn't care less about the political vote.

Some Sunday evenings Gladys and I used to go to Lyons Corner House which was a very lively place. The only snag was that we had to leave by half past nine and really it was only beginning to warm up then. We used to get there about eight o'clock. We'd choose the cheapest thing on the menu – egg on toast or sometimes beans on toast. And then we'd perhaps have a glass of shandy or if we were very daring and we weren't too hard up we'd have a glass of wine.

There used to be two women who went there regularly. We saw them every time we went. They were about thirty – very sophisticated type of women – hair cut very short. They used mascara, lipstick, and a dead-white powder. I suppose in a way they looked like clowns, but we didn't think so.

The most daring thing was that they used to smoke cigarettes. All right, Gladys used to have a puff now and then up in the bedroom that we shared. I'd keep cave and we'd open the window and flap a towel about if we thought anyone was coming. But to smoke in a public room – and not only that, they used long holders too, like Pola Negri on the pictures – we thought was the height of sophistication.

We used to try to get a seat near the band if we could because it gave a sort of cachet. Everyone tried to get there. It was an eight-piece outfit.

After we'd been going there about half a dozen times we got to know some of the players and we thought they were marvellous. They had a kind of uniform of black, very tight-fitting trousers with a red stripe down the side and red jackets with black facings. And we found them very attractive-looking indeed. And of course we were flattered that they took any notice of us.

Two of them in particular we had our eyes on. Fortunately

we didn't each have our eyes on the same one. Gladys was keen on the one who played the drums, and the one who played the piano I thought would do all right for me. That is if we ever managed to get out with these two remarkable young men.

One night they began calling out to us asking what tunes we'd like them to play – and that was something that sort of made you feel somebody.

I forget what sort of numbers were popular at that time or how we knew they were. I suppose the errand boys were our disc jockeys then, because whenever a hit tune came out all the errand boys would be riding about on their bicycles whistling it.

I used to like the soulful sentimental numbers like *You Were Meant For Me* – romantic things – not like these pop things they have now which seem to be full of hidden meanings. You don't know whether it's an exercise in sex or whether it's a song.

Anyway after we'd chosen a few tunes, a waiter came over with a note from one of them – I don't know whether it was the drummer or the pianist – asking if we could meet them one night.

Well, you can imagine Gladys and me; we were in a seventh heaven thinking that these beautiful bandsmen had actually invited us out. We sent back a note by the waiter saying that we'd meet them at five o'clock on the next Wednesday. We said five because that would give us extra time to do ourselves up and make ourselves look attractive.

And then Gladys said to me, 'On no account tell them that we're in domestic service.'

So I said, 'Well, they're bound to wonder what we do because we have to get in at half past nine.'

We sat there searching our brains. First of all we were secretaries to someone or other and we were doing night work or then we were looking after an art gallery at night.

I said, 'They won't believe anything like that at all, Gladys, so it's no use coming out with those cock and bull things.'

At last we settled on a story that we were cousins. We didn't like to say we were sisters because we were so unlike – and her mother was an invalid and we had to be back at half past nine because the person who looked after her wouldn't stay any later. It sounded a bit thin but it would do.

But after all this planning and scheming we got a horrible shock. There we stood on the corner where we'd arranged to meet at five o'clock and when they came in sight a couple of more insignificant-looking creatures you've never seen in your life.

In uniform and sitting down they looked marvellous but out of uniform and standing up they were simply ciphers. Both about five foot four. We towered above them. And they were wearing horrible flashy light-blue pinstripe suits, gingery-coloured shoes and trilby hats. You've never seen anything like it in your life.

I was horrified to think of all the work we'd put in night after night to get this couple to take us out.

Gladys whispered to me, 'Let's get them in the flicks as quick as we can so that nobody sees them.'

This we did. And while I was sitting there I couldn't help thinking of all the young men you read about. The favourite novelists at that time were Elinor Glyn, Ethel M. Dell and Charles Garvice. And I don't know where they found the type of men that they wrote about: the kind of he-men and yet chivalrous with a kind of power over the women so that they made them do what they wanted. I'd never then nor since met any men like it.

Mind you, all these wonderful lovers on the films Rudolph Valentino and Ramon Novarro – they were just pasteboard lovers, weren't they? I could never understand women raving and going mad about Rudolph Valentino and sending for his photo. In any case who wants a man that you've got to share with a load of other women?

I used to wish that you could find an Englishman who was a sheikh. And I used to think that with the shortage of men there was it would be nice if a man could have three wives like sheikhs did. You could all take it in turns to be number one wife, couldn't you? I wouldn't have minded waiting my turn at all. But Englishmen have got neither the inclination nor the stamina.

Later when I was married I used to think it would be fine for women to have two husbands because you really need two husbands. One to go out to work for you, to support you and keep a roof over your head, and one for pleasure, because the one that does all the work is too tired for pleasure.

Anyway, there I sat in the pictures getting some sort of pleasure by watching sheikhs because I knew that these two we'd got with us were no sheikhs. One and six to go into the pictures and a fourpenny ice-cream and that was the extent of what they were going to spend on us.

When we came out we separated. Gladys and I had agreed on this. We had a kind of code whereby if we'd got two young men who might be dangerous if they got us on our own we would never separate. When we used to go to Hyde Park and walk around with guardsmen there we'd never separate. Nothing would have induced me to be alone with a guardsman. I mean, they'd got no money to start with so you could be sure they were on the lookout for some pleasure that costs nothing.

But these couple of weeds – they didn't rate.

When we got outside my pianist steered me down a dark street. Nowadays of course you can't find a dark street. I don't wonder people do their courting in broad daylight – it's either that or not do it at all.

Well, we walked down this dark street and all of a sudden he stopped and started getting sort of het up – breathing heavily all over me just like a lot of other young men I'd had – puffing, panting, and pawing was about the extent of their repertoire. And it's so ridiculous, isn't it, because if you want someone to start patting and pawing you, you obviously have got to have some feeling for them? You've got to think that you'd like them to do it. But when you've met someone for the first time you can't have much feeling for them at all, so why should they think you have?

It just shows the colossal egotism of a man, doesn't it – that he thinks every woman he takes out wants him to drape himself round her neck and be affectionate to her? They don't even give you time to get to like them. And the last straw came when he suddenly burst out laughing.

'What are you laughing at?' I said.

'Oh,' he said, '1 can't help thinking of the girl I'd arranged to meet tonight. I wonder how long she waited for me?'

Well, I was simply livid. What a thing to say to me. That he'd arranged to meet another girl and then ditched her at the last minute.

Just at this time we'd come to an Underground station so I said, 'Do you mind excusing me for a minute – I want to go to the lavatory?'

I hated saying it because we never mentioned things like that.

He said, 'All right then.'

I said, 'You wait at the top of the steps. Don't move, will you? I shan't be long.'

So I went down – bought a ticket home and left him standing there. Just like his other girlfriend waiting. And I kept laughing in the train just as he had. Men!

8

THE ONLY TIME I nearly lost a girlfriend over a boyfriend was when Gladys and I shared one between us. We picked him up one Sunday afternoon in a Lyons' teashop; the place was so crowded that the only empty seat was next to us and he came up and said with a rather attractive accent, 'Could I please sit down at your table? It is the only place available.' From the way he spoke we could tell he was a foreigner.

Gladys, who was never at a loss where the opposite sex was concerned, got into conversation with him. We found out that his name was Jan de Beers and that he came from Amsterdam. He assured us that he was no relation to the diamond people of that name. He needn't have bothered, because what with his appearance, which was by no means smart, and the fact that all he was having was one bun and a cup of tea, we knew that already.

We were rather wary of foreigners, particularly Italians and Spanish, because we knew they came from very hot countries and the passion and heat went together. We felt they wouldn't respect English girls. I know it sounds trite now, the word Respect, but it was a word that was continually drummed into us so we took notice of it then. If we met foreigners from the more temperate climates like America, New Zealand, or Australia these were quite all right because obviously they were more affiliated to us. They had the same colour of skin as we had. In those days, as far as we were concerned, anyone who had got the same colour skin as we had got must be all right. Mind you, we thought Indians were all right because they had lovely coffee-coloured skins and there was always the chance that they might be sons of rajahs or princes or things.

Opposite the place where we were working the house had been taken over by the Government for Indian students; we never got any further than waving to them at night because of the caste system. They were educated enough to know that we were only servants and that it wasn't going to do their prestige any good to be seen out with people like us. Apart from his bun and cup of tea Gladys and I weren't surprised to find that this young man was no relation to the diamond people because we never found any young men who had got any money and we never expected to. For us it was enough that he was good-looking. He said he had been a steward on a ship that had gone backwards and forwards to and from South Africa but that the last time it had docked in Southampton he decided not to sign on again but to work in England for a while. I was a bit sceptical about this explanation because he seemed young to be a steward. I assumed that by the time you got to be a steward you would be at least twenty-five to thirty.

Anyway he went on to say that he was working in a factory on night shift, the nature of his work he was unable to explain for some reason or another. Gladys said, 'Is it secret work?'

'Well, no,' he said, 'it's not secret.' But he wouldn't explain what it was. He said his English wasn't good enough. Later on I suggested to Gladys that he was probably only a night watchman. She got annoyed with me when I said that so I knew that she had already begun to like him – she always got annoyed if you made any detrimental remarks about a fellow whom she had begun to like. Even if he had a face like the back of a bus and no money or education this meant nothing to Gladys if she took to him.

The moment Gladys met a young man she never failed to start weaving a romance around him. This I found strange considering how hard-headed she was and the fact that she came from Stepney; maybe Stepney was a place where you have got to weave romances and have a strong imagination because it was the only thing that enabled you to live there.

Anyway this Jan de Beers took us to the pictures that night. He sat in the middle and bought us identical boxes of chocolates and after that the three of us went out together about half a dozen times.

The occasion of the rift between Gladys and me was when she said that she was going to meet this Jan on her own one night. This meant I was to go out by myself. I was up in arms immediately, not because I had fallen for him but because I felt she was assuming that he would prefer to go out with her rather than me. And I couldn't see that he'd shown any inclination to do this.

Mind you there were the intervals when we each had to dive off to the loo and when I was gone he may have said something to her. I'll agree he never said anything to me when she had gone to the loo, but that doesn't mean to say he hadn't said anything to her to the effect that a twosome might be better than a threesome.

As regards looks there really wasn't much to choose between Gladys and me, as neither of us was particularly good-looking. The only thing was with Gladys coming from Stepney as she did she could usually produce some very colourful stories about her life down there. This Jan was a very sober and sedate young man; he neither drank nor smoked and he told us he was a member of the Dutch Reformed Church, which meant nothing to us, in fact Gladys shocked him because she said if the Church needed reforming there wasn't much hope for the congregation. But perhaps because he was such a very moral young man he used to lap up all these lurid tales that Gladys would tell about life in Stepney.

I used to think he was a spy compiling a book in secret about the social life of the working-class people in England: telling of the seamy side of life, and showing it wasn't such a land fit for heroes as everyone was led to believe.

However the funny thing about this fellow was that he didn't really understand what Gladys was saying. Although he thought her tales were dreadful and immoral they didn't have the same implications for him as they did for Gladys. For instance she used to tell about a woman who lived next door to where she did. This woman's husband was a deck hand and whenever he came home it seems he got her in the family way, but while he was away she took on another man and they used to sleep together in the same room as the children. Jan said, 'Oh, how awful,' and you could tell he was shocked. Gladys said, 'Yes, wasn't it, but you see they had no other rooms.' Jan thought it was awful them being immoral but Gladys thought it was only immoral because they were doing it in the same room as the children.

Anyway I reckon I must have made my feelings pretty plain about Gladys and him going out without me, because on our very next evening out she told me he was bringing a blind date for me.

I wasn't very pleased about that because my experience of blind dates was that you really needed to be blind to be seen out with one. With all the surplus females about any young man who couldn't get a girl by himself had something wrong with him. But I was wrong, for when we did meet my blind date he wasn't too bad. Charley his name was and he was an under-steward with the P&O line. This Jan was lodging in this Charley's house and Charley's mother was Jan's landlady.

When we met, Charley said we were all invited to a party because his mother had just got married again, the third time this was, and the party was in a large room in a pub. I wasn't too keen on parties as not only did you meet a lot of people you'd never met before and you fervently hoped you were never going to meet again, but whenever we went to a party we'd got to leave by nine-thirty just when things were warming up, which killed everything stone dead. Still we agreed to go. When we got there it was like all other parties, the usual seething mob of people meeting for the first time in what they think is a convivial atmosphere and feeling they've got to add their quota to it by drinking, laughing, singing, and talking, and putting on a complete change of personality from what they have in their own homes.

Anyway we were taken up and introduced to this Charley's mum and her third husband. I was astounded that she had ever been able to get one husband never mind three. I'd never in all my life seen such a fat woman; she must have weighed fully twenty stone. She'd got arms like legs of mutton, several double chins and great mounds of flesh in front. The appendages that nature had endowed her with were resting somewhere down on her waist. This was mainly because she wore nothing to stop them. In those days bras were never heard of for the working class; you wore a thing called a liberty bodice which was very much like a strait jacket. All it did was suppress the mass of flesh and make it flat, but if you didn't wear one at all, which she didn't, anything you had was left hanging around in all directions.

And yet all this massive weight was supported on the most slender pair of legs you have ever seen. She had lovely legs and she only took size four and a half in shoes so really if you just looked at her feet and legs, which was maybe all her husband intended to do, it wasn't too bad.

84

The new husband wasn't at all a bad-looking specimen. You couldn't help wondering what he saw in her, whatever induced him to marry this mountain of flesh. Leaving aside the physical difficulties of any amorous interludes, there was the fact that she had already got through two husbands. I'd be very suspicious of anyone who had got through two husbands.

The first one had succumbed to an attack of influenza and the second fell off a ladder. He was a window cleaner. Later on, after I had got to know Charley's mother a bit better, she showed me photos of her first two husbands. Unlike her third, they were certainly no oil paintings – a fact that she freely admitted.

The first one, Henry, had a very short upper lip like a rabbit. I've seen children like that and it looks quite attractive on them but when they're grown up it looks ludicrous. She said to me, 'Henry not only looked like a rabbit; he was like one in bed, too. Our first night together could have been a fiasco because on our honeymoon when we got to the boarding-house they were full up and the only way they could make room for us was to turn their children out and give us their room. Unfortunately the beds were bunk beds.' 'Still,' I said, innocently, 'even from bunk beds you could hold hands.' 'Oh,' she said, 'Nature had endowed him so generously that I held a lot more than that. Oh, yes,' she said, 'and we managed. Of course I wasn't as fat as I am now but I weighed all of fourteen stone even then.'

I decided it was time to change the subject. 'How did you meet your second husband?'

'It was very soon after Henry died, in fact I met Frank at the funeral. He was a friend of Henry's and he came round several times to console me for my loss. I've always been the sort of woman who must have a man around to cook and clean for; I'm lost without one. So we got married after four months. But then,' she added, 'I know that Henry would have wished it.'

You know, it's peculiar to me how many widows always seem to know just what their departed husbands would have wished for them. I knew a woman once who never listened to a word her husband said nor ever took his advice when he was alive, but once he had removed himself from this world (via a rapid descent from a cliff) based the rest of her life on what he would have said or thought. Being as she never gave him a chance to express any thoughts in life I wondered how she knew what his wishes were now he was dead. Anyway to get back to Charley's mum.

'How did you get on with Frank, your second husband?' I asked her. 'Ah,' she said, 'he was a sad disappointment to me. No go in him at all, no stamina. He was always on about what a friend Henry had been to him, how much he missed him and the comfort he felt in being in Henry's home amongst all the things he'd loved. I don't know whether he included me amongst the things Henry had loved. If he did, perhaps he felt he shouldn't show any enjoyment at using Henry's property. No,' she said, 'Frank was always so mournful, in some ways it was a happy release when he fell off that ladder cleaning windows.'

I don't know if she meant a happy release for her or

for Frank. I was interested to know how she would make out with her third husband but I got fed-up with waiting around for Charley to come back from his trips at sea. And so did Gladys because her Jan and my Charley teamed up on the same boat together and calmly sailed out of our lives. I mean it's all very well saying absence makes the heart grow fonder but it's got to be given a chance to get fond to start with. Otherwise it just makes the heart grow accustomed.

9

PHILOMENA KEMP WAS the parlourmaid in my first job in London. She was engaged to be married and her young man was named Fred Keatings.

One Sunday, on Philomena's afternoon off, it was raining cats and dogs so Mrs Bowchard, the cook, asked her what she was going to do. Philomena said, 'Well, I'm meeting Fred but I don't know what we shall do, it's raining so hard.' Neither of them wanted to spend money by going to the pictures or suchlike because they were saving up to get married. So Mrs Bowchard said, 'Well, bring him in, that'll pass the afternoon away and by the time you've had tea maybe the weather will have cleared up and you can go for a walk. That way it won't cost you anything.'

So in Fred came and we all sat down to tea. There were six of us altogether. Gladys the under-housemaid, Jack, our sort of handyman, the cook and me, and Philomena and her intended.

Philomena was busy making her trousseau. Everybody

made a trousseau in those days and you tried to have as many of everything as you possibly could. Philomena had bought no end of linen for her bottom drawer. Six of everything, sheets, pillowcases, towels, and she was making three of everything for underclothes. I don't know why three – one on, one off and one in the wash I suppose. Mind you, if you were well-to-do you had far more than three of everything.

Still, not only the rich had. I remember my mother telling me that when she was in service one of the maids had a dozen of everything. Calico of course they wore in those days. But, mind you, she'd been engaged for seven years, so I presume she had the time to make them. Philomena hadn't, so she was making do with three.

Crêpe de Chine was all the go in those days. There weren't things like nylon or tricel or any of the man-made fibres that there are today. *Crêpe de Chine* was a lovely silky material, and at this particular time Philomena was making a nightdress of it. It was an eau-de-nil colour – a very pale green – with a low neck. I remember how daring we thought it was. None of us except Jack, who was a widower, had ever been married and we didn't know anything about that kind of thing. She was sewing bows all down the back of it at intervals of about four inches which I thought was rather daft.

Philomena was the youngest of sixteen children. Her mother had worked through the alphabet and that's why she got such a peculiar name.

She had a photo of her mother in the bedroom that she

shared with the housemaid, and she was such a prim-looking little woman. You wouldn't have thought she'd had one child, let alone sixteen.

Mind you, people did look more prim in those days. No make-up, your hair done up in a bun and your clothes covering almost every portion of your anatomy. You were bound to look prim. Nowadays so much shows that almost everybody knows what they're buying before they even sample the goods in the marriage market.

Once I said to Philomena, 'Fancy your mother having sixteen children. She doesn't look the type.' She said her mother was so fertile that if she'd only kissed her father sixteen times in sixteen years she would have had sixteen children. I suppose she knew what she was talking about. She said her mother was a very religious woman and that she always read the Bible every night before she went to bed. She certainly needed to get strength from somewhere I reckon.

Anyway back to the kitchen.

After tea Philomena got on with her sewing while we sat around making ribald remarks about the low-necked nightdress. And then we chanted that little rhyme, 'Change the name and not the letter, change for worse and not for better.' Her name was Kemp and his was Keatings so she wasn't changing the letter; she was embroidering the initial K on everything. It's one of those ridiculous, old wives' tales but I partly believed it. When you are that age you believe anything.

While we were going on in this way Jack, the handyman, suddenly said, 'I well remember my wedding night.' So we all pricked our ears up expecting either some very sentimental recollection or some very erotic one, preferably the latter as far as I was concerned. And the others were, too, I expect because we didn't go much on sentiment in the servants' hall.

'Yes,' he said, 'we got married in a registry office. We had very little money and we couldn't afford a proper reception. We hadn't anywhere to live or any furniture, so we stayed on at my mum's. We had a bit of a "do" in Mum's front room and all the neighbours came in with crates of beer and bottles of wine and there was dancing and whatnot and about midnight I was blind drunk. I took my boots off and got into bed. I woke at about six and I suppose I was still fuddled from all the booze I'd had. I got out of bed, felt under it for my boots, put them on, crept downstairs in the dark the same as I'd done every morning, put the kettle on, made myself a cup of tea, picked up my sandwiches and went off to work. It wasn't until I'd been at work about an hour or two and saw all my mates grinning at me and then kept on hearing them say, "Old Jack he looks tired today, doesn't he? I wonder why Jackie looks so tired? He must be working too hard. You should take a holiday, Jack." Then it came to me that I'd got spliced the night before. Well, when dinnertime came I ran all the way home. I'd never got there so quick in my life and I had three lovely courses for my dinner.'

Well I didn't know whether to laugh or cry. It bore absolutely no resemblance to the lovely bridal nights that I read about in *Peg's Paper*, where the husband is so chivalrous to his bride that he carries her over the threshold and then they have a lovely candlelit dinner together. And then they go upstairs and the blushing bride goes into the bedroom, undresses on her own, puts on a lovely chiffon nightdress and sits up in bed with a bow in her hair and then a sort of veil is drawn over the rest of the proceedings. So old Jack's account of his wedding night was like nothing I'd ever heard before.

And Fred Keatings, he sat there quiet all the time. Never a glimmer of a smile while Jack told his story. He was such a sober, respectable young man. He sort of oozed sobriety from every pore and I could see that he took a very poor view of Jack.

Mind you, Jack knew that Fred Keatings didn't like him. He couldn't resist making sarcastic remarks to Fred. One thing that used to annoy Fred particularly was old Jack asking if he was related to *The* Keatings, the makers of the famous powder that killed bugs, fleas, and beetles.

For my part I wouldn't have minded a bit being related to The Keatings or having some shares in their concern because they must have sold gallons of their powder. I know in my own home, owing to the slummy places that my dad had to go, doing his painting and decorating, we always had enough fleas to fill a dozen circuses. My mother used to wage a perpetual war on them. She used to powder the bed with Keatings so that every time you made it a miniature sand storm went up.

Perhaps Fred had an aversion to fleas. But one look at

Fred and you knew that no self-respecting flea would ever bite him. He was such a poor specimen of humanity that he'd never provide a happy hunting ground. He was a wet, phlegmatic kind of person. You could never visualize him showing any kind of emotion let alone a passionate one. Yet Philomena used to say that he was very passionate, that she had to fight to keep him on the straight and narrow. But he certainly never showed any signs of that in the servants' hall.

He used to sit there drinking a cup of tea with his little finger sticking out at right angles and his hands were so pale they looked like white slugs to me. He used to make me shudder. And then there was the nicety of his speech and his obsequious manners. I suppose these were the result of his job. He was a shop assistant in a very large draper's stores and he'd been doing this kind of work from the time he left school. He started to work in a gentlemen's hatters as errand boy and he gradually worked his way up till he was a sort of chief shop assistant. His greatest ambition was to become a floor walker. Personally I thought it was a terrible ambition.

They don't seem to have floor walkers these days. I suppose the aisles are so full of people there wouldn't be enough room for a floor walker to manoeuvre. But in those days with less people around and less money around, it was more the well-to-do who patronized these kind of shops and I well remember the floor walkers in their frock coats – snootiest people imaginable, they seemed. But they were very discerning.

They could size up a customer the minute they saw one. The deference in their manner when greeting somebody who looked as though they hadn't a ha'penny to their name but they sensed came from a titled family! Whereas someone smart with probably a lot of money would only get slight attention. They graded their civility according to the aristocratic position of their customers.

To listen to Fred's conversation you would have thought that all the nobility and gentry came up to Fred's counter in preference to anybody else. He'd say, 'Who do you think I served this morning?' Nobody cared of course but you knew that you were going to hear just the same. 'Why,' he said, 'Lady Betty – now there's a real lady for you.' What an unreal one was I never did find out. 'She gave me such a sweet smile.' What were you supposed to say to that? Then he'd say, 'The Duke of Walton was in trouble over a tie for his young nephew, the Honourable Peter. The Duke is elderly, you know, and he doesn't know what young men like today.'

Well, I thought poor old Philomena.

Personally I felt that if he was the last man in the world I would never have married him though the time was to come, believe me, when if I could have got a Fred Keatings I would have been glad. I thought I'd had it. Once or twice I thought I was going to be on the shelf – for ever.

But nevertheless at that time when I was only sixteen I was full of hopes. I wasn't going to marry anyone like Fred Keatings. I could see Philomena, slippers all ready for him. 'Well, dear, what kind of day did you have today?' And there she'd have him trotting out about who he'd served and what they'd said and the sweet smiles they'd given him. Day after day and year after year it would go on till he got to be a floor walker. Then it would be ten times worse. That's what I thought at the time.

But alas for Philomena it wasn't to happen.

There they were, all set, introduced in the proper way – no picking up – making all her trousseau with her bottom drawer ready, and Fred Keatings with his eyes upon becoming a floor walker and a model of propriety. Yet they were never to marry.

A few days after our kitchen party Fred Keatings, that model of rectitude, was arrested for indecent exposure. And that was a heinous crime in those days.

Mind you, it happened to me once or twice and I always laughed. I just couldn't help it. It looked so funny. Nowadays they are given medical treatment but they didn't do things like that then. They just got put in prison. Fred was sent down for two years because it was discovered that it was his third offence.

And poor Philomena. She went right round the bend – off her head – and she had to be put into a mental home. Talk about losing your head for a man. Today people would probably take the thing in their stride and the wedding would have happened. But then of course it was a disgrace and anyone who was disgraced became a social outcast, an untouchable. It shows too the importance a girl attached to getting married, so that losing a boyfriend could send her out of her wits.

10

THE NANNIES I particularly remember were from the time when I was a kitchenmaid in London. The people I worked for had a married daughter with three children living with them, which meant having both a nanny and an under-nurse. We disliked all nannies, nurses and under-nurses because they were neither flesh, fowl, nor good red herrings as you might say. They were not the kind of people you worked for and they were not of the kind of *us*. They were sort of out in limbo. Perhaps this wasn't true of the under-nurse. She got the worst of both worlds – not rated by the nanny and we classed her as if she were, as she had to be with the nanny. Yet even nanny wasn't one of *them* because she had to work for her living. I suppose in fact nannies didn't have much of a life, but we thought they did, and we disliked them intensely in the kitchen because we had to prepare different meals for them.

The nurse would come down and tell the cook what menu she wanted, and cook would be awkward and bloody-minded because as far as the cook was concerned only one person should give orders and that was the madam. But if the nurse thought that the day's meals were unsuitable for the children she'd come down and say so and others would have to be cooked specially for them. Then when the nurse went upstairs cook would explode and I got the blast. No, we didn't like nannies.

But as I say the under-nurse really had a horrible time of it because she was stuck up there with only that nurse for company and she had to work hard. There was a day nursery and a night nursery; the under-nurse had to scrub both these out each day and when I say scrub I mean scrub, because in those days there was linoleum on the floor. She had to do the washing for the children, the napkins and the rougher stuff, while the nurse did the dainty things.

I hadn't been at that job long when another baby was due, which made it four children. Never in all my life had I seen such a carry-on about somebody having a baby. I wouldn't have believed people could have made all that fuss. To begin with there was a shuffling round of rooms because our nurse didn't take children from birth – so another nurse arrived, took her room, and ours had to sleep in with the under-nurse. And the room had to be redecorated which was another thing that annoyed our nurse because, as she said, it hadn't been redecorated for her who had been with the family for three years, so why should it be redecorated for someone who was only going to come for a month or two. I said to the cook, 'She'll reap the benefit when the nurse has gone, she'll go back into it.' I should have kept my mouth shut. The cook picked up the carving knife and made a gesture and uttered something too horrible to repeat.

Anyway two weeks before the baby was expected this nurse who took babies from birth was installed – so you can just imagine what it was like in the household: two nurses and an under-nurse, three kids and one on the way. That was when I made up my mind never to go to another place where they had children. With the hostility that there was between this new nurse and the old one, you could have cut the atmosphere with a knife. Yet they had to be outwardly polite. It was 'Good morning, Nurse' and 'What do you think of this, Nurse?' But the old nurse wouldn't let the new one do anything so she just sat around getting in the way, waiting for the baby to be born. And what with the fact that the baby was a week late as well – she was left hovering for three weeks. The only one that benefited was the under-nurse because our nurse joined forces with her against the other one, so for once in her life everything that she said and did was right. This changed of course as soon as the other nurse went.

Then after the baby was born, yet another nurse came – a wet nurse to feed the baby, you see. She had a month-old baby of her own but she came in several times a day to feed ours as well. I must say I found this procedure most peculiar at the time, but I didn't after I'd had my first baby because I had so much milk I used to chuck the stuff down the sink although I was feeding my baby. People talk now about how good these cans of food are. They start ramming them down the baby's neck when they're two months old and they say how much healthier babies are for it. I had so much milk that I fed my first child until he was eleven months old and he never had anything else. It was so cheap and we were hard up, and it was clean and hygienic. I never had to bother about washing out bottles and as I say I had so much of it I often wished I knew another baby that I could have given it to. I didn't realize then that you could go up to a hospital with it and that they're always glad to accept it.

But this woman got paid for it. I used to wonder, did her own baby suffer? If somebody had to go short it obviously wasn't going to be the baby that she was being paid to feed. She only came for a month though – after that the baby was put on to one of these patent foods.

But during those weeks what with two nurses and an under-nurse and a wet nurse, absolute pandemonium reigned. I didn't help matters because one day I had to tell our nurse that the wet nurse had arrived.

So I said, 'Daisy's here.'

She said, 'Daisy?'

I said, 'Yes, you know, Daisy the cow, who comes to feed the baby.'

Talk about lese-majesty. She drew herself up to her full height. 'How dare you,' she said. 'Associating the sacred rights of motherhood with being a cow. It's nothing like being a cow at all. It's giving life to someone.'

She went on like that for about five minutes. I went down to the kitchen and told the cook, looking for sympathy.

'Serves you bloody well right,' she said.

I suppose it did.

Nowadays, as I say, mothers don't like feeding their babies. They think there's something distasteful about it. It's these damned little cans of food – that's what it is. If they had to do what we had to – put stuff through the sieve and mash it all up once we put the baby on solids, they'd feed them. I used to sigh for the days when I fed them myself and had no bother at all.

Then of course well-to-do ladies didn't feed their babies because it ruined their figures. It spoiled the shape of their bosoms. Perhaps it doesn't nowadays because of the bras they've invented. But I really don't believe that anyone can feed a baby, not for any length of time, and still have the same-shaped breasts afterwards.

And again at that time no well-to-do lady who went to a lot of social functions was going to be pestered with having to feed her baby every three to four hours. Why did they pay out money for nurses and under-nurses if they were going to be tied to the baby themselves?

The whole paraphernalia of their way of having a baby simply amazed me and Gladys. Her mother had had swarms of kids. Madam stayed in bed a whole fortnight. A fortnight! My mother used to stay in six days and Gladys said her mother used only to stay three days. Who was going to look after the other mob? Her mum used to come down and start scrubbing and it never did her any harm. And then she fed the babies as well as doing all this work in the house.

They say once you start work you can't feed the babies, but it's all my eye and Betty Martin. Of course you can – especially if you drink a lot of beer like Gladys's mum did.

And I don't blame her for drinking it either. If I was living in Stepney and had had swarms of kids I would be drinking beer all the time too.

Having a working-class baby was a very casual thing. You never made many preparations beforehand. Naturally you got a few clothes in for it and the midwife would call some time near the date. Nowadays too you get all this talk about new psychological methods and a husband being in the room at the time of birth because it's good for him – it gives him a kind of feeling of oneness with the mother and baby. They talk this high-faluting rubbish as though it was a new thing. In working-class households the husband always was there. My dad was – there was only him and the midwife. And he was kept running in and out with kettles of hot water because we didn't have any hot water laid on. We only had an old sink and an outside lavatory. So Dad was in the room nearly the whole time. And so were other working-class husbands.

The way they talk now as though that's why all babies are wonderful and that's why there's such a feeling of affinity between parents because the father was in the room when the baby was born – it's all rubbish. There was no psychology as far as Dad was concerned – it was sheer necessity – lack of money. And as soon as the baby was delivered Dad did everything, the washing – and there's a whole lot of washing after you've had a baby – and clearing up. He took over and the next day Mother would do as much as she could from the bed. Like preparing the vegetables. Anything she could do with her hands.

So when Gladys and I saw all this paraphernalia of having a baby as though it was something out of the ordinary, we wanted to spit. People had kids like a bet on the Derby – once a year. Well, why not if you can? And why was there all this fuss? It's not as if having children was going to alter their lives. Where I was in service the mothers upstairs had nothing to do with their children. They saw them once a day. They never had the pleasure of them.

Surely to have the pleasure of children is to be with them when they're young and to give them the love and security that they can only get by knowing that their parents care about them. It's only then that you get something in return. It's nothing to do with money. I don't think these children were lucky – only in as much as they had all the food, the clothes and the toys that they wanted. But they weren't lucky in having the kind of things that we had in our home without money.

I often think, looking back, and because of the letters I've had since I wrote *Below Stairs*, that we were the fortunate ones. I've had letters from people who were children in these opulent homes. They say, 'We never had such a good time. You think because you were down there slaving away that you were the only ones that suffered, but you weren't.' One person wrote and said that she only saw her parents once a day when she went in the drawing-room at five o'clock after tea and that she had a cruel nurse, but felt so divorced from her parents that she was frightened to tell them how unkind she was, because she was sure that her parents wouldn't have done anything about it except to tell the nurse what she'd said, and that she would be even more ill-treated. So you see, she wasn't any better off than children in an orphanage who are given every material comfort but haven't got some one person who really cares about them.

But the nurse where I was working – in spite of the fact that we didn't like her – wasn't like that. The children thought the world of her – so she must have been kind to them and given them love. I could tell by the way they used to run after her and climb over her. So although to us she seemed stand-offish and snooty she couldn't have been so bad.

But what sort of life did she have to look forward to? They just lived for a time on borrowed affection. Then the children they had taken care of went away to boarding schools and they'd have to take another job and start all over again. What sort of existence was that? Although life below stairs was rough and ready, at least it was life. The rigid social divisions in any of the houses I worked in were generally carefully defined. You knew your place and you kept in it. You worked and played within certain limits and under certain terms and rules and it was seldom that these were ever broken.

I only remember one place where this happened. The goings-on there would have interested even Mr Sigmund Freud.

11

IT WAS AFTER I'd been in service in London for some years, I thought I'd like to be a bit nearer home for a change, so I came back to Hove and I worked for a Mr and Mrs Bishop.

It was a very peculiar kind of house in many ways. No one could say that they belonged to the gentry.

Mrs Bishop was a woman of about sixty who made herself up to look about thirty-five to forty and she did it extremely well. She led her own life – at the weekends at any rate, which was the only time they were in Hove. The house was filled with young men – young in comparison to her that is – and it was a very lively forty-eight hours indeed, though for most of the time Mr Bishop wandered around looking like a lost soul. But then he had his own little bit of fun during the week.

He would come down on his own to satisfy his particular aberration. And that was to inveigle one of the maids into his bedroom late at night when they were wearing their hair curlers. Then she'd sit on his bed while he fingered her curlers. That's how he got his pleasure. He was what I believe they nowadays call kinky.

Another expression you hear today is 'permissive society' as though it's something new. But the only difference from when I was young is that now this permissiveness applies to everybody – not just the rich. There's always been a permissive society for the well-to-do because if you'd got rank or wealth it excused a multitude of evils. Also rank and wealth gave you the opportunities and the facilities to be permissive.

Take the kinky Mr Bishop. If he hadn't had a house of his own and servants and hadn't been able to come down and live alone with us in the week, he wouldn't have been able to indulge in his peculiar habit of wanting to feel the servants' hair curlers.

The working classes couldn't have done it. Well we didn't have that peculiar taste. I suppose some of us had peculiar tastes but how, when, or where they could be satisfied is beyond me.

And although the maids used to profit by this peculiarity of Mr Bishop's by gifts of chocolates, stockings, and theatre tickets, we were contemptuous of him. We thought that somebody with his money and education shouldn't indulge in these footling pursuits. That they should be above such things. We weren't to know, as people do now, that this kind of obsession couldn't be helped.

Among ourselves we used to make fun of him and, when Mrs Bishop wasn't around, wouldn't give him the respect that we would a normal employer. We never used to call him Sir and we would grin like hyenas when we met him.

Well, what more could he expect? But we liked him because he was pleasant, gentle, and kind.

Yet after I'd been there about six months something happened that made me change my opinion of him completely. And it will show you how much I respected him when I tell you I never said a word of what I found out to another soul. And this at a time when precious little of interest or excitement came into our lives, so that we had to embroider the more mundane things to make them dramatic.

It happened one night when I was coming home from a dance. I'd been with a boyfriend who didn't bother to escort me home when he found that there wasn't going to be anything on the end of it. After an evening out I always believed in making the position clear. You might just as well be friends when all's said and done because some of them used to get very annoyed when they had taken me home and all they got for it was a goodnight kiss. I learnt this early on when one night I was being escorted back from another dance by a fellow. I didn't take him right to the door – fortunately. We stood in a turning parallel to it and he began to get extremely frisky. He was about twice my size too. Well, I got very nervous – matters were getting out of hand – so I said to him I needed to go to the loo. So he said, 'Where?'

'I live the next turning to this. I won't be long.'

He said, 'You won't come back.'

'Won't come back?' I echoed, making as though I was simply dying to come back. 'Of course I'll come back.' I said, 'You'll wait here for me, won't you?'

So I dashed to the house, bolted the door and got out of that awkward situation. The excuse of going to the loo has been very useful to me on occasions. Perhaps that's why they called it a convenience. That's a bit of a deviation from my story but it accounts for me coming home from the dance alone.

As I was saying, I was walking by the Hotel Metropole on the seafront, when who should be coming out of the hotel but Mr Bishop and a woman. She looked about forty – nothing particular about her – quite plain – and plainly dressed, too. It was all very embarrassing because I didn't know what to do. I'd almost bumped into them. Mr Bishop said, 'Good evening,' and she looked a bit odd. I muttered something and that was that.

But the strange part was that in the normal way when I'd got in I would have come out with it about seeing Mr Bishop with another woman. But I didn't. I don't know what restrained me then because I was quite young and hadn't got much sympathy for anyone who deviated from the norm.

I'd almost forgotten the episode when two or three days later I received a letter from a stranger and on reading it, it transpired it was from this woman. She asked me if I would go and see her at her flat in Brighton. 'Well,' I thought, 'it can't do any harm to see her.' So I went on my day out.

The first thing she asked me was, 'Have you said anything about seeing me with Mr Bishop?'

I said, 'No, I haven't said a word. It's strange really because we do talk about him.'

So she begged me not to either to the other maids or

to Mrs Bishop. I told her of course that I wouldn't. She didn't have to implore me – I wasn't going to say anything anyway. Now of course I wouldn't. I didn't want to spoil things for other people. Then she went on to tell me a story that could have come straight out of a novelette.

Her name was Dora and she'd been a housemaid with Mr and Mrs Bishop many years ago. There was a son of the house who seduced her, got her into trouble and landed her with a baby. As soon as Mrs Bishop heard of it, although she knew it was her son who was responsible, she dismissed Dora without a reference. So as well as the stigma of an illegitimate child, she had no money and no chance to get another job. I asked her why she didn't sue the son.

She said, 'Well how could I? By the time I'd had the baby he'd been sent to Australia as a ticket of leave man for forging his father's cheques. In any case it would only have been my word against his and I wouldn't have stood a chance.'

It was always the same then. It was always the girl's fault if she got into trouble. Nobody ever blamed the man. It was considered natural for a man to pursue and to get everything he could and if he could find a girl that was muggins enough to give it him – well, she deserved what she got.

She went on, 'I knew he was a bit of a ne'er-do-well but he told me he was emigrating to Australia and that he'd take me with him. But it was the old story. He didn't care about me any more when I told him I was pregnant. And the next thing I knew was that he'd gone.'

So I said, 'What did you do then?'

She'd written to Mrs Bishop asking her to help out with money but she never got a reply. She'd managed to borrow a bit but when the baby, a boy, was two months old she was at her wits' end. There seemed to be no hope at all. And then out of the blue Mr Bishop wrote to her and suggested that they meet.

She said, 'He came to see me and was marvellous. He paid off my debts and set me up in this flat. And he's looked after us both and paid for the child's education. But the reason you saw us together is that now my son is married and I'm on my own Mr Bishop comes to see me once a week on a Wednesday night.'

Well I couldn't help grinning thinking about what might be happening.

So she laughed, too, this Dora, and she said, 'I know what you're laughing at.'

I said, 'Well, I wouldn't really have asked you outright – but it's the hair curlers.'

We both went off into fits of laughter about this.

Anyway it transpired that half of every Wednesday night was spent fixing and playing with hair curlers. They used them on each other – not only on their heads but in other places as well.

'Don't you get fed up with that sort of queerness?' I said. 'After all, it's hardly the kind of thing that you expect to find in normal society, is it?'

So she said, 'Well, if normal society means that when you take a wrong step people treat you like dirt as I was treated, give me abnormality every time. Apart from this oddness

Mr Bishop has always been kind and generous to me. He knows I've got another man friend and he doesn't mind in the least so long as he can come here Wednesday nights.

'For him,' she said, 'it's an oasis of quietness after the racketty life that his wife leads.'

I never saw her again after that, and although I never mentioned it to a soul I used to wake up at nights and roar with laughter thinking about an elderly man and a middle-aged woman experimenting half the night with hair curlers.

But it showed, didn't it, that it couldn't really pay you to step outside your own social circle. If you did it was a near-certainty that you would be the one to get hurt.

Mind you, even flirting with the trades people could have its dangers as I was to find out.

12

WHEN I WAS in domestic service we didn't have any super-markets but we certainly had super service and super food. No shopping had to be done by the cook. Occasionally if she went out in the afternoon she would look round the shops to see what new things were in. But she didn't have to. The tradesmen called every morning. By tradesmen I mean the owners or managers or their assistants. They would take the orders, talk about any special things they'd got in and then later the errand boys arrived and delivered. The cook would make them come right into the kitchen and she'd examine what they'd brought and if it wasn't right there would be no question of making do – she sent it back. For instance if you ordered a particular slice of rump steak or fillet steak or fillet veal and the cook thought that it wasn't up to standard, she wouldn't keep it; the errand boy would have to take it away and come back with something that she thought was.

Incidentally Albert my husband was a butcher boy at one

time; he said that often when they took something back all the butcher did was chop a lump off the end and return it again and it was always accepted.

When the tradesmen called all the under-servants, the under-housemaid, under-parlourmaid and me, we used to try to make ourselves look as nice as possible. I noticed that the under-housemaid and under-parlourmaid always seemed to be below stairs at these times. The under-parlourmaid had a legitimate excuse to be down because of the butler's pantry being there, but the under-housemaid's work was upstairs.

The under-parlourmaid used the butler's pantry for washing up all the silver – none of it was washed up in the scullery. The silver and the afternoon tea things were washed up in the pantry. Then there were cupboards to put silver away in and green baize covers to fit everything into. There were shammy leathers galore for polishing and special cloths and papier-mâché bowls so that the silver didn't get scratched. All very different from the stinking old sinks I had out in the kitchen.

But back to our hovering around the tradesmen. It was really an absolute waste of time because the ones who called for orders were either already married or, if not, were far too old, and the errand boys that came with the things were always much too young.

The butcher's boy at my first place in London was the only errand boy I really fancied but unfortunately it was all too obvious that he didn't fancy me. He was tall and hand-some like an Adonis and he had wavy hair. He was a real heart-throb. Agnes the under-parlourmaid used to vie with me for his favours. She was a sentimental girl and had a real crush on him, but like me she was wasting her time. All her sweet words and languishing looks were repeated ad infinitum by the servants wherever he went. He had marvellous opportunities so you can be sure that he shopped around for the best and the easiest. I adopted a sort of a hard-to-get attitude, completely ignoring this Adonis – I thought that this might intrigue him enough to make him become interested in me. But what a hope! I might have been empty air for all the notice he took of me. When I think about it now it's obvious that if you want to intrigue somebody you've got to look intriguing yourself and I certainly looked far from intriguing. Not many kitchenmaids could look intriguing, especially just after they've done the kitchen range.

When I later became a cook I acquired a position of authority over the tradesmen and at one time I did contemplate a life of bliss with a fishmonger. Well, not a life of bliss exactly but life with a fairly substantial income. I know that sounds a materialistic approach to matrimony, divorced from the sort of romantic ideals, but unless you're so violently in love that time and motion cease to exist, money does count. I mean, in exchange for a nice home, nice clothes, and good food you can look at any man through rose-coloured glasses. Well, I thought I could.

This fishmonger, Mr Hailsham, certainly needed looking at through rose-coloured glasses. He resembled nothing so much as one of the large cod fish that he used to bring – considered very suitable for servants' meals, being very nourishing, you know. His flesh was dead white and it was always cold, and he had tiny little expressionless eyes. But he had a very flourishing business. He used to supply far larger establishments than ours was and, according to Mr Hailsham, his father and his grandfather supplied the gentry and nobility. He showed me photos – so I suppose there must have been some truth in what he said.

The only time Mr Hailsham showed any sign of animation was when we were talking about fish. You might think it was difficult to wax poetical over a salmon or a turbot but Mr Hailsham could. He used to go to the market every morning and he'd start off on a great rigmarole about looking into their mouths, studying their scales and their tails – ecstatic he used to get. And that's why he got to look like his fish. You see, he lived, thought and breathed fish.

He was about twenty years older than me so not unnaturally I assumed that he was married. One really cold morning I invited him in for a cup of coffee – what with the fish being so cold and him looking so cold I took pity on him. And he got a bit forthcoming. I found he lived with a brother and a sister and none of them was married. I kept on with the recipe of a cup of coffee and after a few weeks he thawed out even more and became quite friendly towards me. Then I commented on the fact that all three of them were still single.

'Oh,' he said, 'my dear mother, God bless her, made us promise before she died to keep together and always help each other.'

'But surely,' I said, 'she didn't mean that you'd got to

look after each other to the extent that you couldn't ever get married? She couldn't have meant that. After all the name's going to die out if you don't get married and with your business so long established you don't want that to happen.'

So he said, 'Well, we've never had any inclination to get married up to now.' And he looked at me in a meaningful way.

At least I thought he looked at me in a meaningful way. I suppose it was a meaningful way – it was difficult to tell with his eyes. He certainly looked at me. So I continued to cultivate him, to sort of get closer to him, though the all-pervading odour of fish that hung around him was hardly an inducement for closer proximity.

Then the other servants said, 'You'll never get him, you know. He's been a bachelor far too long and his sister looks after them both too well.'

This was a bit of a challenge. It's amazing what a determined woman can do. I find even the most rigid and intractable of men lose their powers of resistance where a woman's concerned. You've only got to look at Adam and Eve, haven't you? – going back to Biblical days. Adam could have refused to bite the apple, couldn't he? The reason he didn't refuse it was because he knew that Eve had already had a large bite out of it and that she'd be banished from the Garden of Eden in any case and he didn't want to stop there without her, so he thought he might as well have a bite too and then they'd both have to go. That's the reason. Not because she really tempted him but because he thought what was the good of the Garden of Eden if he was living in it on his own?

Mind you, I had to put in an awful lot of spadework to bring this Mr Hailsham up to scratch. Cups of tea and home-made cakes, and listening to long dreary anecdotes about the fish business and Mr Hailsham's acumen and judgement and that he'd made it such a flourishing concern – not his brother. You see Mr Hailsham did the buying and the orders and the brother did the selling in the shop, and according to Mr Hailsham it was the buying that was the main thing because if you didn't buy well you wouldn't sell well. There was something in that, I think. Then when his sister was ill I made nourishing dishes for her – egg custards and things like that. It paid off eventually because there came the fateful morning when Mr Hailsham said to me, 'Don't call me Mr Hailsham, call me Cyril.' Cyril – I ask you – anyone less like a Cyril I've never met in my life. And this was the prelude to Cyril asking me to go out with him on my next evening off. I agreed, though with some trepidation. I wondered what he'd look like when he was dressed up. But never in my wildest imaginings did I visualize the figure that I saw waiting for me at the end of the street when I went out. Talk about Beau Brummell and Beau Nash rolled into one. He was wearing spats and he had a flyaway bow, yellow shammy-leather gloves and a silver-topped cane, and he was holding a bouquet of flowers. Well, I nearly died of mirth. Talk about seeing Mr Hailsham the fishmonger turned to Cyril the fop. And yet despite this he still had the odour of fish pervading him and it was hard to associate this sort of Beau Brummell with the fishy smell.

Anyway I went out with him on several occasions and

eventually it led to an invitation to tea with his brother and sister. His sister was something of an invalid – she enjoyed bad health. They lived over the fish shop – quite a lot of rooms they had because there were two floors, but they were the kind of rooms that gave me claustrophobia. They were so heavy, crowded, and ornate. They had flock wallpaper in a dark red colour and I felt as though the walls were pressing in on me all the time. And they were full of things that had belonged to 'dear Mother' and were kept for sentimental reasons. 'Dear Mother' had collected these little small pieces of china from wherever she went on holiday. There were things from Margate and Ramsgate and Broadstairs, little bits of crest china, a whole cabinet full of them, with antimacassars on every chair and stuffed birds in cages. And wherever you sat the beady eyes of these things followed you.

I must say though that they were all very nice to me. I'd been a bit scared about meeting the sister. After all, everyone had said she wouldn't let any female get her claws into either of her brothers. She was charm itself. 'Miss Langley – or may I call you Margaret?' That sort of thing. And she showed me over the flat. No, I was welcomed with open arms. It wasn't until a bit later that I realized the full Machiavellian plot that was being hatched over me. It was only disclosed when Cyril and his brother had gone out to get a drink and to bring in a bottle of port for her and me. She was drinking it for medicinal purposes and I would be drinking it for never you mind what. They hadn't been gone five minutes before his sister came over and put her arms round me, and if there's anything I hate it's a woman mauling me around. I'm not that keen on some men mauling me around, but a woman – never.

Then she said, 'Oh, I'm so very glad that Cyril's found a friend like you. You know one that can cook well and look after a house. We need another pair of hands here – now that I'm an invalid. Cyril and Harry, they're so fond of their food and only the best is good enough for them. You being a cook will appreciate that.'

And she went on, 'I can't tell you how glad Harry and I are that Cyril's found you.'

I was absolutely dumbfounded. As far as I was concerned we were only in the very early stages.

So I said, 'Aren't you going ahead a bit? We don't know each other all that well yet.'

'Oh, but you will,' she said. 'I know Cyril's made up his mind. He talked to us about you and about how domesticated you are. We shall all live here so happily together.'

I nearly passed out. Here had I been thinking it was me that was doing the chasing and I'd swum straight into the fish-net. You can just imagine. I mean married to old cod's eyes Cyril. It mightn't be the realization of a maiden's dream. But taking on Cyril, his brother, his sister, and all the Victorian impedimenta as well – well it was a life sentence that I wasn't prepared to serve, I can assure you. Maybe a ready-made home and material comforts had to be paid for but not to that extent. Just a bloody unpaid housekeeper.

Then I visualized the night I first went to bed with Cyril. Those two would be holding their breaths and conjuring up the kind of orgy that they thought he and I would be conducting in our bedroom. And for all his lifeless exterior he might have been like that. These late starters often begin where others finish, on the assumption that now they've got the property they might as well make all possible use of it because they may not have what it takes that much longer to do it. So forewarned was forearmed. As soon as I possibly could with politeness, I dropped off inviting Cyril in for cups of coffee. And I certainly left off sending any delicacies round for his sister. And it was fortunate that at that time my mother became ill so that my evenings were spent going round and looking after her.

13

AFTER ALL MY efforts to get and keep a man I eventually found one right on my own doorstep. Somebody who'd been calling twice a day since I'd been cook in the house – the milkman. His name was Albert – Albert Powell.

I'd never thought of him as a possible husband because he was five years older than I was and I guessed he must be married. Most working-class men were married at his age, particularly with all the surplus girls there were about then – so I thought he'd already been snaffled.

I've written a lot about catching a young man and it may seem as though I never thought of anything else and that I was blatant in my efforts to get hold of one. But what you should realize is that everyone was the same then. The upper-class girls were just as keen to get married as we were. But they could do it in a more civilized manner. They had coming-out parties and went to theatres and deb parties and were introduced to men. The whole idea of being debs was that they should meet young men and get married.

Then of course more than now. In any class marriage was a career for a girl because on any level there weren't the jobs for women. But our efforts had to be blatant. The only way we could get young men was either to meet them at dances or pick them up in the cinema or in the parks. So although this method may seem vulgar it was the only way open to us. We would have liked to have been properly introduced to them but if we'd waited for that we would have waited for ever.

Another reason why I thought that Albert was married was that he always wore a ring on his wedding finger. Not many married men wore rings – never mind single ones. When I got married and I found that it wasn't compulsory for married men to wear wedding rings I promptly left mine off as well. This was one inequality between the sexes that I could do something about.

Ever since I'd been cook at that house I'd enjoyed seeing Albert the milkman, because he was always so lively and cheerful no matter what the weather was like. He'd always have a laugh and a joke – all tradesmen were like that. I used to see him regularly twice a day. But in all that time he never showed any kind of endearment. He never tried to get over-friendly with me or to kiss me, so I never really thought about him that way at all.

When I look back on it I often think that the reason that we got on so well, when we did start going out together, was because we'd seen so much of each other and knew each other so well that I didn't have to keep trying to impress him the way I'd done other men. And I don't have that horrible sick anxiety when I'd said goodnight and made a date to meet again as to whether he was going to turn up the next time. I knew I would see him the following morning.

Admittedly I didn't feel any transports of love but then I didn't want to feel them any more. You know, each time you met a boy you felt, 'This is the one I've been waiting all my life for,' and then you'd realize that if it was you'd have to wait alone because he certainly didn't feel that way about you. I was glad that was over. And we got on fine. He was kind and he was generous. Every time he met me he'd have a box of chocolates under his arm and it was the best seats in the cinema and sometimes even a taxi back home and flowers. He was a kind and generous man and I liked him very much. And he liked me.

We went out several months and eventually we decided that we liked each other enough to make a good basis to get married on. It might sound a bit cold-blooded now but I don't think it was. I mean we liked the same things. Perhaps there was not a lot of emotion – but I'd had emotion. This being up in the heavens one minute and down in the depths the next with a man is no basis for marriage. Because while you'll put up with it before marriage, you don't afterwards and that's the way the rows start. Then again he liked drinking and so did I. So we agreed that we'd get married.

As we'd got very little money between us we decided on a registry office because it was that or a white wedding with all the trimmings – and it doesn't matter who you invite, you never please everybody. You spend a fortune on guests and they go back and compare it unfavourably to other weddings they've been to. I know because I've done the same thing myself. Again, if we'd have had that sort of wedding we'd have had to buy our furniture on the never-never. So we decided on a registry office and furnishing our home for cash. The only thing we did get on hire purchase was the piano. And we had to have one because in those days no working-class home was complete without a piano. Neither of us could play it. I used to bang things out with one finger, same as I do with typing.

It was just as well that we had nothing else on the never-never because we hadn't been married six months when Albert lost his job. There was a dole by then but it wasn't very much money and he was out for a long time. He was just about to go on public assistance which meant having that horrible means test. It was a very lean time for us and the piano had to go back because we couldn't keep the payments up. This was terrible, you see, when they came to take it away. It had to go out the same way as it had come in – through our basement-flat window. It took so long to get that piano out that quite a crowd collected to watch and I felt so mortified. They must all have known that it was going back because we couldn't afford to pay for it. Albert said, 'Don't worry, maybe they'll think it's going to be tuned.' I didn't know whether to cry or laugh, so I said, 'Let's hope none of them heard that remark. It's bad enough them watching our piano going because we can't pay for it, without them knowing that I married a bloody ignoramus.' I didn't mean it of course.

When we got married we couldn't afford a honeymoon,

but Albert had a week off work and we went around looking at London. We used to enjoy going to the various markets. Like the Caledonian Market – it's gone now – where you could get practically anything. One of the stallholders there who spoke in a most cultured voice told us that after he'd put his stall up in the morning he'd wander round the others buying up stuff which he himself then sold. When you get that kind of thing happening there must have been bargains.

Another interesting one was Berwick Market. It was one of those where you could have your wallet stolen as you entered it and buy it back as you left the other end. I'd been there several times with Gladys. It was lovely. They had stalls all down the centre of the road with awnings on them, and the shops on either side had got their awnings out too – it was like a covered market. But it was no place to go alone – that is if you wanted to look at the shops. You had to go in pairs. Not because you might be assaulted physically but because of the strong, intense verbal barrage you were subjected to even if you stopped to look in the shop windows.

Every shop had a tout in the doorway – generally a man – and the moment you stopped and looked they started talking and gradually edging you inside. And once you were inside you were very lucky indeed if you got out without buying something – and generally something you didn't want. Part of their sales technique was to get you right to the end of the shop so that you couldn't slip out. Then it was talk, talk, talk.

I remember once being in one with Gladys. They were

selling her a coat. Normally I reckon I'm a person that can get a word in edgeways but I couldn't. Eventually I burst out, 'If you didn't keep up such a running commentary I might be able to tell my friend whether it suits her or not.' So the salesman whispered in my ear, 'You know, if the boss doesn't hear me talking all the time he thinks I'm not trying to make a sale.' It probably was like that too. If you showed any signs of leaving the shop without buying anything the entire family came in – the proprietor, his wife and any odd relations they'd got there. They would stand there and utter those obvious insincerities like, 'Oh, it's lovely, it makes you look years younger. It's just your colouring' – things like that – and you had to be more than strong-minded to resist their blandishments. We didn't. Gladys got a coat that she didn't want and hardly ever wore. But I hand it to those traders, although I got exasperated at their methods, they knew how to run a shop. After all, the idea of running a shop is to sell things – and they did. And although you vowed you'd never go back – you did.

Another market Albert and I went to was in Leather Lane. The day we went there there were two Indians selling mysterious ingredients from the East. One was an aphrodisiac to give you the sexual urge, well we'd only just got married so we hadn't found any dearth in that line, and the other was a powder – a panacea to cure all ills. They seemed to be doing more trade with the aphrodisiac than the panacea which must have proved something about us British.

Farther down the Lane there was a large crowd around two men. One of them was tying the other up in chains. He took his time but when he'd done it he asked any member of the audience to step up and try to extract him. A man stepped forward – part of the act I suppose – and he tried but couldn't do it. Then the chap who'd done the tying up said, 'Of his own volition and completely unaided he can get out of these chains in sixty seconds. But, before I start, I solicit your coppers.' And he went round with his cap. You should have seen the audience melt – and when the sixty seconds were up and he was out of his chains, there were only six people left and we were two of them. This again must have proved something.

Our two-roomed basement flat in Church Street, Chelsea, may have been a good address but it badly needed re-decorating and of course being newly married we were a bit houseproud, so Albert said he'd have a go at it. He'd never done anything like it before but I told him it was child's play because of my father and brother being in the game; the way they used to do it, it looked like child's play. Like all jobs which real experts do.

Albert decided that he'd paper the kitchen first. You never saw such a mess as we got into. None of the paper seemed to match up. We cut it wrong lengths and the pattern looked terrible. Then it tore because he put too much paste on it – and the last straw was when he stepped into a bowl of size and it shot all over the floor. Eventually it got done and we didn't think it looked too bad. We thought that the fact that the pattern didn't match didn't matter if you didn't examine it too closely. And when you're just married you only look at one thing closely.

Anyway I decided that it wanted a couple of pictures hanging on it – and I didn't want just reproductions that you can buy anywhere and that everybody has. I wanted something original. And I'd read in the paper that morning about an exhibition in one of those galleries in Bond Street. The pictures were by a new artist and the critic had said that the prices were within the reach of all. I imagined I'd get something for about a pound but when I got there, there was nothing under five pounds and the five-pound ones were only the size of a pocket handkerchief. I'd never seen such pictures, gloomy old things they were, dark and sombre scenes – all greys and browns. You felt as though you were in the depths of woe when you looked at them. I expect they were good but I thought they were miserable to look at.

I wandered around about three times. I wasn't going to buy anything. I decided that at first glance. But it looked a bit bad going in, giving it the once over and going out again and I wanted to look knowledgeable. Then one of those assistants came prancing up to me on the balls of his feet and said, 'Can I help you? Is there anything you fancy?' So I said, 'Well, no, they're all too expensive for me.' And I said, 'They're not very pretty, are they?' Well, by the look of horror that came over his face you'd have thought his trousers had just dropped down. 'Pretty,' he said. 'Pretty! Madam we sell paintings, not Christmas cards.' Well, I thought, that was a stupid way of talking. After all's said and done you want something that's going to liven you up, don't you? You don't want to look at the walls and think death's gradually coming ever nearer. We know it is, but we don't want to be reminded of it. Imagine getting up in the morning, going into the kitchen and looking at two of those things. It would drive you straight back to bed again. Anyway I felt very small, mortified, and ignorant at the whole thing – but you can't expect to know everything, can you?

Albert and I were very happy and comfortable in Church Street – though I did sometimes wonder after struggling all those years to get married what all the fuss was about. It didn't seem to me that it was anything to get over-excited about. Mind you, I wasn't any Lady Chatterley and Albert wasn't the gamekeeper. Somebody lent us a book very soon after we were married which I thought jazzed the thing up a bit. The *Kama Sutra*. I suppose you could call it Variations on a Theme. I put it on the bedside table – Albert's side – but as everything went on in the same old way I suppose it never got read.

I found that having a milkman for a husband was a far different proposition from having a milkman when you were in domestic service when you only saw him for a few minutes every day. There were quite a few disadvantages attached to being married to a milkman in as much as he did two rounds a day and for the first round he had to be up at half past four in the morning because he started at half past five. And then he'd come back at ten o'clock for his breakfast and then go off for the second round and back at three for his dinner. That's why of course we got used to such irregular meals and why we're so irregular now – in fact now we've got regular irregularity, if you know what I mean.

Being newly married I couldn't bear to think that he got up on his own at half past four so I got up too, made him a cup of tea and gave him a snack and a sandwich to eat on the round. But fortunately before my enthusiasm had waned he told me that he'd sooner do it on his own. What I think made him decide was that I'm one of those people who, the moment they get out of bed, start talking. I feel like that in the morning. I do more in the morning than in the evening. And I think Albert used to get fed up with my chit-chat. So when that stopped all I had to do was to get breakfast ready for him at ten o'clock. His wages were three pounds five and any commission he got for finding new customers, so we managed quite well. Our rent for the two rooms was fifteen shillings a week.

He went on his rounds by horse and cart. He had a very spirited animal with a disconcerting habit of rearing right up on its hind legs. Albert reckoned it had been a circus horse at one time. He really loved that animal. Agatha was her name but he called her Aggie. And he always used to be talking about Aggie. I got quite jealous. I felt at times he thought more of Aggie than me.

He had a terrible time one day in the winter when there was a thick fog. Aggie was so used to the rounds that while he called at one house she'd walk on to the next one. This particular day walking on in the fog she lost her way and Albert lost his horse and cart. He went wandering around asking people if they'd seen a milkcart anywhere. It took him over an hour to find them. But, jealousy apart, she was a lovely horse. When Albert used to stand on the footboard

with the reins in his hand I used to think that he was Ben
Hur driving his chariot. I used to feel really proud of him.
Him and his Aggie.

His round took him to Maida Vale where some of the
ladies of the night used to live. When he used to knock
on the door once a week for the money they used to be in
bed recovering from the rigours of the night before. Some
of them used to offer to pay in kind, but of course as we'd
only recently got married he insisted on the money. Other
customers used to treat Albert as a bookmaker's runner as
well as a milkman. He'd take the slips and the money and
pass them over to a bookmaker he knew.

One disastrous day a woman gave him five bob to put
on a rank outsider and when Albert came in he handed it
to me. 'I'm not putting that money on,' he said, 'the horse
won't win – it can't possibly.' Well, the damned thing came
in and we had to find three pounds out of our own money to
pay her. It was a financial crisis for us.

Many of the customers used to ask Albert to do odd jobs
for them – shifting furniture, rolling carpets, even fitting
tap washers. We used to get a lot of things that way. Many's
the piece of furniture Albert's come home with on the cart
and, later, toys for the children. People used to make a
friend of the milkman then. They saw him every day and
sometimes twice a day. It isn't like now where you give a
regular order and he leaves it on your doorstep and if you
want anything different you put a note in one of the empty
bottles and you only see him when you pay him.

Also of course not many women went out to work – not

working-class women anyway. Most of them had big families and the women used to get lonely. They'd ask Albert in for cups of tea and talk to him as a friend. Many a woman would look at him with a worried face and say, 'Milkman, I've clicked again,' meaning they were pregnant. 'What am I going to do about it?'

Of course Albert didn't know. The only things he knew about was the same old things that everybody knew – hot baths, Beecham's pills, Penny Royal, or quinine – and none of these are any good. I know because I've taken them myself. I remember going to a doctor once to see if he would give me anything and he said the only thing he knew was, 'The hair of the dog that bit you. And,' he said, 'it costs you nothing and you enjoy it.'

That then was Albert's life as a milkman. It was a full life and he enjoyed his work. I think that's what's the matter today with men. Everything is a production-line job with nothing to relieve the mundane. It's no fun. So the only reason they work is for money and when the money isn't right they strike for more. But when you like what you do and take an interest and a pride in it money isn't so important – you're happy – so you're contented. Albert was contented and so was I. It was a very good start to our marriage.

14

OF ALL THE places that we lived in in London Chelsea was the best. Of course it was very different then to what it is now.

The King's Road was a busy one, but none of the people using it looked like they do now – there was none of this Carnaby Street atmosphere. Maybe by the standards of those days the people seemed eccentric – well, the artists did – but there was nothing like the queer collection of bits and pieces that you see strutting up and down encumbering the road.

Some of the artists were indistinguishable from anybody else. Some of them walked around in velvet jackets with flowing ties and beards and perhaps long hair, but at the same time most of them were serious artists. And you felt that their clothes were a necessary corollary to their way of earning a living. They didn't obtrude as though they were some sort of freak society as they seem to now. Most artists have been priced right out of Chelsea now that it has become a popular neighbourhood.

Of course even in those days you'd get the show-offs. Some of them came into our local pub – especially the less serious artists. They'd come in with their clothes and hands all painty and they'd lounge about at the bar talking about perspectives, high-faluting stuff like that. The Chelsea trippers as we used to call the people who came into Chelsea as voyeurs used to buy their drinks under the mistaken impression that they were hobnobbing with some future Turner or Landseer. We used to laugh to watch them being conned.

You could see them lapping it all up. I think they were titillated by the thought that they were mixing with the loose-livers. No doubt some of them were. There's been loose living from time immemorial, hasn't there? But people that are living loose don't go around shouting it from the house tops. It was a fallacy to think that those indulging had it written all over their faces. Many a person who looked the epitome of respectability might have been living the most lurid life.

The artists had their models and they used to come into the pub with them, but whether they were living in immorality you couldn't tell – and you couldn't ask them, could you?

The people there seemed to go with the surroundings. Of all the boroughs I've lived in, Chelsea was the only one that seemed to have a communal society. Everybody seemed to mix easily. The business people, the shopkeepers, the artists, and just ordinary working-class people like us – you didn't feel a class difference somehow. You were some sort of whole.

The nearest we got to any kind of intimacy with an artist was with our landlord and landlady who lived above us. But he wasn't a real artist, he was a sort of amateur dauber. He worked in an office all day and only painted in his leisure time.

Mr West was his name. He was a very short man, and like a lot of very short men he was pompous and wanted to throw his weight around. A lot of short men feel that you're going to overlook them or that you think they're not real men. For instance, he'd been married eight years and they'd only got one child although they really wanted more and Mr West used to consider that this was some kind of reflection on his virility. It wasn't true really because I've known quite a few extremely insignificant men with huge families. I think their wives sort of carry them forward, if you know what I mean.

Anyway this Mr West used to paint his wife in the nude. He painted her naked body and then he'd put different heads on it. He wanted me to sit for him in the nude, too. He promised he'd put a different head on me, too, so that nobody would actually know it was me. That's what he said – there may have been a more obvious reason of course. But Albert wouldn't let me. He wouldn't have minded me sitting for the head and putting it on some nude figure, but for me to be the nude figure, he just wouldn't stand for all that. I didn't really mind. I didn't particularly want to do it. Personally I think any female looks better with some clothes on. Mrs West certainly looked better with hers on. Very few females really look at their best without.

Today nobody takes any notice of nudity – not only in paintings but in real life. But even then to paint nudes was considered a very sort of way-out thing to do. No doubt that was the reason Mr West did it. He wanted to prove something. Real artists don't have to bother whether they look Bohemian or not but Mr West wanted to look like a Bohemian because he wasn't a real artist.

One of the next-door neighbours Albert and I had was a Russian, Boris Borovsky – I forget how it was spelt but that was his name. His wife was English – her name was Stella and a very nice person she was too.

Boris used to wear one of those Cossack hats all the time so that everyone could see he had affiliations with Russia and in the privacy of his own home he used to wear his shirt outside his trousers. He said all the Kulaks did that. I didn't even know what a Kulak was – and I don't now. He was always talking about what a wonderful place Russia was since the Revolution and I couldn't help wondering sometimes why, if it was that good, he didn't go back, but I reckon he knew where he was best off.

I don't know what sort of work he used to do – accounting I think it was. It was something whereby he had to work a lot on his own, so when he came home he was very glad of an audience. He'd talk about the heroism of the Russian workers. He was a great one for the Russian workers. Then he'd say, 'Look at the sailors on the *Potemkin*.' I'd never heard of the *Potemkin* – I didn't even know what it was. It was a long time before I realized it was a battleship. Apparently they had a mutiny on board.

He used to compare the sailors on the *Potemkin* with our sailors that mutinied under Captain Bligh. He said that there was all the difference in the world because the sailors that mutinied on the *Bounty* only mutinied to better themselves, whereas the sailors that mutinied on the *Potemkin* mutinied to better the lot of the workers in all Russia. I hadn't got the courage to tell him that I didn't know anything about the country, that my knowledge of Russia could have been written on the back of a halfpenny stamp. I knew they'd had a Revolution and that they weren't much good in the First World War, that they'd departed from the battlefield with great speed, and that was about all. But when he used to talk like this he used to talk to *me* personally. I thought it was wonderful that someone should talk to me like this and tell me these things. I thought that I was really seeing life on a grand scale.

When I was in domestic service all the maids were interested in was the bits of scandal from upstairs. They didn't come down and talk about culture. Nobody cared about culture then. Mind you, while I listened I used to think that his wife must have got bored with that kind of conversation. I suppose with me you couldn't call them conversations. I mean, they were more monologues in as much as all my part was, 'Oh, really! Well, fancy that! You don't say!' and other equally inane remarks.

Boris had also got very strong views about the place of women in the home. He thought that women's only place was the home and that their whole purpose in life was to look after their husbands and children. They'd got five. In fact he reckoned that half the trouble in Russia was because of the Czarina. That if the old Czar had knocked her about a bit, instead of letting her have her own way in everything, there'd never have been all this trouble with the old mad monk Rasputin.

He said, 'Don't you agree?'

And I said, 'Yes, you're right.'

I'd never even heard of Rasputin. If he'd asked me I'd have said he was some West Indian chap. But I didn't ask questions – just agreed. Because that way I got more conversations. Sometimes he used to act the big man with me. 'I'm master in my house,' he'd say. 'What I say goes. Stella's mind is as my own.' Good solid masculine horseshit.

Little did he know that Stella had a secret life that was nothing to do with him at all.

This Stella was a good milliner and she used to make hats for quite a few of the neighbours. She could have earned very good money in a shop, but he wouldn't let her because he didn't want her to be financially independent. But while he was at work she used to make hats in secret and there used to be a man call regularly. She said he came to buy the hats. Maybe he did but he stayed a very long time doing it, and I wouldn't have thought you had to draw the bedroom curtains to look at hats. No. It's my opinion Stella had an interesting side to her life if Boris had but found out. It's just as well he didn't know as much as he thought he did.

When I got to know her better, we were talking one day and I mentioned Russia.

She said, 'For God's sake don't you start on about that bloody place.' Then she poured out her feelings of boredom and frustration to me.

She said, 'If you'd known Boris as long as I have you wouldn't sit there listening open-mouthed and looking at him as though he was the Great Panjandrum himself like you do. I've heard it all so many times I feel as though I'm going stark raving mad. Why doesn't the stupid bombastic nitwit go back to the Russia he's always talking about, where the workers are so free and where he says they can divorce their wives so easily and where there's free love?

'Love,' she said. 'He doesn't know what the word means. He thinks it's that five-minute exercise I have to suffer with him once a week.

'And the bloody farce is,' she said, 'he doesn't know a thing about Russia – only what he's read. He left there when he was three years old and yet he talks as though he was responsible for the Revolution. I'm sick and tired of it.'

After this outburst I explained to Stella about my lust for knowledge and culture, and how although I was enjoying marriage I got a bit bored. So we thought it would be a good idea if we could collect a few young mothers and have a kind of a club and meet once a week.

We got together about six or eight mothers and we arranged to meet in each other's houses in turns. The idea was that whoever's turn it was should study some political, social, or cultural event and speak about it and then we would have a debate. In that way we thought we'd be able to give our brains a sort of turning over. We thought that we might create some kind of miniature Fabian Society, but instead of promoting socialism alone we were going to promote culture as well. For a while everything went well and then one day someone hadn't had the time to prepare anything, so we hadn't got a subject to discuss and before long this was happening with increasing regularity and the whole thing degenerated into the usual stupid women's chit-chat about what little Mary said, what little Johnnie did, what they'd told the teacher or what new thing they'd bought for their home. And there was nothing we could do about it.

Looking back on it I suppose it was rubbing shoulders in the pubs with the artists and thinkers that made me feel I could change the set ways of women's lives. I couldn't. But eventually I did change my own and I think it was living in Chelsea that opened my eyes to my own educational deficiencies. I wouldn't have missed it for the world.

15

ALBERT GOT CALLED up for the Forces in 1941 – they were having anybody then, as he said.

I'll never forget the day he went because his sister and I saw him off. She was weeping buckets of tears but I wasn't weeping at all. Not because I wasn't sorry to see him go – of course I was – but one gets philosophical about these kind of things. It wasn't as if he was going into the front line. He went into the RAF and not on flying duties – posted to Yorkshire. I was left in London in the front line with three children.

We were living in Lewisham at the time and we had one of those shelters in the garden – Anderson shelters – corrugated-iron things. You dug them down in the garden. And we'd had raids night after night without a break. So he was lucky – he was leaving that. Mind you, Albert never used to turn a hair. He used to sit in the shelter totting up his day's work. He was a marvellous person to have during a raid because he literally didn't feel anything. It wasn't that he was consciously being brave and heroic. It just didn't worry him. He thought that the probability that a bomb would fall on our particular little shelter was mathematically impossible. But I used to dread it because the railway used to run at the back of our garden and the sparks from the trains used to shoot up in the air. Why we troubled about blackout I don't know.

We had no end of incendiary bombs. We were supposed to rush out and throw earth all over them. But Albert would never come out because he hated talking to the neighbours. We spent hours and hours in that shelter in the garden. I used to be afraid; I'm not going to pretend I wasn't. I was deathly afraid, night after night, but I had the children to think about and if you don't show fear the children are not afraid either. So I couldn't show fear for their sake. If it had been just me and Albert I'd probably have been a quivering wreck.

But when they called him up I didn't really see the sense in staying in London with three young children on my own. My parents were still living in Hove and they told me they could get me a house down there to rent since a lot of people were leaving because of what they called the hit and run raids. They weren't really that. I mean there was nothing to hit in Hove, but the German planes unloaded their bombs there because then they had more chance of getting back. As a matter of fact it was funny that the house we eventually lived in there got more damage than our place in London.

But of course I'd lived in Hove as a girl – and in a way

it was like going back home for me. We also used to take our annual holiday there but we had to give that up – not because we couldn't afford it; after all we could stay with Mum. We couldn't afford the consequences. You see we'd taken our holidays in June, July, and August for three years running and our three children were born in March, April, and May. Well, if we'd kept on going down Lord knows how many children we would have had.

We couldn't really afford three children anyway. We should have stayed at two but as the first two were boys I was dying to get a girl and the doctor said to me when I told him this, 'Feed your husband up on pickles, spices, and onions and then you'll probably get one.' So I did that. I rather like spicy foods anyway. Albert didn't know what I was doing. But it was all rubbish because I still got a boy, and yet everyone had told me it was going to be a girl. All those wise women said, 'Oh, you're carrying it different this time – it's all round instead of being stuck out in the front.' People tell you this nonsense when you're carrying a baby, and they are mainly spinsters who do so. It's a funny thing to me that people who have never had any babies always seem to know more about it than those that have. To my mind that doctor should have been struck off for giving me that load of cobblers, or I should have had my head examined. I don't know which.

Anyway it was a boy, born on a Sunday. All my children were born on Sundays. I don't know whether that means anything – all were boys and all weighed eight and a half pounds. You couldn't have anything more monotonous than that, could you?

With the last one, when Albert went down to get the mid-wife in the morning she said, 'Oh, I'm just going off to church.' Very annoyed she was that I was having it then. What did she expect me to do – wait until after the service? It's true, I did – until after the evening service, much to her annoyance.

It took ages. It always did take me ages to have children. Some people can drop them like a hot cake. I do think they're lucky. The first of my babies took nearly three days to arrive. When they do it's never worth it. I mean, when you see them, little miserable-looking red objects they are, bawling away and all the relatives come and say; 'Oh, isn't it lovely!' and even a mother's eye can see it isn't lovely at all. I like them eventually but I've never been blind to the fact that they don't look anything at all to start with. But your relatives tell you it's marvellous. Then they say it looks like Albert or it looks like you and you don't want it to look like either of you because you know perfectly well it won't get on in the world if it does.

At any rate when this one was finally born it was about seven o'clock in the evening. I suppose the midwife did think it was a long time in coming but she didn't think it was as long a time as I did. When it arrived she said, 'It's an-other boy, Mother.' And I said, 'I don't care if it's a monkey so long as it's got here at last.' She was really taken aback. I could sense that and she said, 'I look upon every child I deliver as sent down from heaven, planted in earth's soil to grow up as a flower.' But she was a spinster and had never planted anything in the ground, otherwise she wouldn't have talked like that.

143

It's all daft, isn't it? This rubbish you read in romantic magazines – Charles Garvice and Ethel M. Dell – as if it was something mysterious and beautiful. It's a revolting business. People walk in and out the room when you're in the most peculiar position, you're looking your worst and you're suffering the tortures of the damned. It isn't a bit like what you read in books. Not for the mother. It's all right for the father – he just sits around.

The reason I had three children was because birth control at prices the working class could afford was only just beginning to come in. The well-to-do have always been able to have birth control either by doctors providing them with things, or with cosy abortions if they didn't work. But all we did was try to be careful. Nobody told me about the 'safe' period. We didn't chat about those sort of things then.

Mind you, I don't think there is any safe period. The Catholics call it Roman Roulette down our way. I'm not one but when you look at some of the huge families that Roman Catholics have, either they wanted a huge family or they kept slipping up badly. It depends a lot on the sort of husband you've got, doesn't it? I mean if a husband can regulate his desires to the safe period it may be all right. But what I know about men, they never regulate themselves. It just depends on how they feel. If they've had a damned good day at work they feel like a kind of a whoopee at night and they don't bother to inquire. Or if you tell them it's not all right they say, 'Oh well, let's take a chance.' They don't have to have them, you see. Makes all the difference in the world.

After I'd had two children I heard about a birth-control place in Ladbroke Grove for working-class women. It was in a very poor neighbourhood next door to the employment exchange; at that time there was a lot of unemployment around and the men used to hang about outside. The premises were a converted shop, and though it wasn't labelled birth-control clinic all the men knew what it was; the women who went there used to feel so conspicuous, we used to slink up to and into the place as though we were doing something really depraved. The men used to grin as you went in – but it was worse when you came out. 'All ready for it now, darling,' they'd say – or words to that effect.

The methods they had then weren't nearly as convenient as they are now. They were somewhat irksome to say the least and you had to keep coming back to be refitted. The thing was unattractive to look at and uncomfortable to wear. And you had to wear it most of the time. I mean you couldn't ask your husband after you'd given him his supper whether he would be liable to require the contraption tonight – it's not a sort of fireside conversation, is it? Anyway people like us didn't discuss things like that – not working-class families. The whole thing was shrouded in gloom and mystery. You went to bed and you drew the blinds and you put the lights out and everything went on in the dark. It was all bound up with the way English people felt then about sex. Even amongst married people it was sort of faintly illegal. I suppose we consider that anything that's nice and that we get for nothing must be illegal. As far as that contraption was concerned, if you went to bed without it and then discovered that it was required, it was either too late or it was the death knell of that spontaneous combustion that the love act ought to be. I mean, you just imagine when you're sort of full of love and somebody nudges you and says, 'Have you or haven't you?' If you haven't, you've got to get out of bed and do all the preliminaries, so by the time you get in again all the emotions you had have evaporated in the cold night air. So that's why we had three.

After Albert joined up I moved down to Hove. My mother got me a six-roomed house for a pound a week. It was cheap even then. Of course we'd not had a house in London and we'd only got enough furniture for three rooms so I put a bit in every room. At least everybody had a bedroom to themselves. The boys thought it was marvellous all having a room each instead of all being in one as they were before.

In spite of the fact that people were leaving the town there still seemed to be plenty about and a fair amount of life considering that it was wartime. And there were the troops, Canadian troops, not American. It was really too marvellous for words after living in London, where the ratio of women to men was about five women to one, to have all these spare men knocking around. And they'd come up and talk to you. They used to spin you the tallest yarns how they'd got ranches out in Calgary and Alberta and places like that and hunting lodges in the mountains. I didn't believe them, of course, though I pretended to. What did it matter – they looked so marvellous in their uniforms?

Our local pub used to be full of them and six formed

themselves into a singing group and they'd entertain us. They're very sort of forthcoming, Canadians; they don't suffer with inhibitions like the English. And they used to start singing and the whole pub would join in. Even Albert when he was on leave liked it and he's not very gregarious. We used to have marvellous times at the local. Mind you, anywhere looks better to a female if there's a lot of men about even although you're not having anything to do with them – just the fact that they're there and they're surplus.

In a way I felt sorry for the British soldiers because these Canadians took the girls away from them. If you went into a pub with one of ours, he'd buy you one half-pint and you'd have to sit and sip it the entire evening. Whereas of course the Canadians could afford to buy whiskies and gin. Can you wonder that all the girls went stark raving mad for them? This business of everybody being so virtuous and all walking on the straight and narrow path – it's only because the opportunity is lacking.

At that time I was doing daily work, charring. With the boys to keep, Albert's money as a corporal wasn't enough so I had to go out. The lady at one of the places I worked kept open house for the Canadians: officers of course not troops: and from time to time these officers would start chatting me up. They loved Brighton. When they had left Canada they thought they were in for a grim time but as they said, it was not only a home from home but it was far more. I remember Madam colouring up a bit when one of them said this, perhaps she thought I didn't know what was going on. Then they'd say how hospitable people were over here and I'd say, 'Yes, but you wouldn't find them like this in the normal way, it's just that the war brings out the best in people as well as the worst.' That was a sort of innuendo.

Well, month after month went by and then one morning I woke up and somehow I could sense a difference in the town, a kind of quietness. I couldn't think what it was. Something seemed to be missing. Anyway I went to work and the lady said, 'They've gone.' 'Who's gone?' I said. 'All the Canadians have gone.' 'They couldn't have,' I said, 'they were here yesterday.' 'But didn't you hear, all through the night those lorries? They've all gone. I shall be absolutely lost having nothing to do for them,' she said. I wasn't quite sure what she meant by that.

I've often wondered though what became of them all. I've never met any who came back. Some girls I knew got married to them and left to join them after the war, and of course there was the quota of unmarried mothers. But Brighton was like a gold-rush town around that time – like Canada had been with the Klondike – one moment it was filled with riotous assembly, with laughter and noise and then it was as if the mines were depleted. Suddenly the men were gone. Mind you, I think the publicans thought the gold had gone too; their trade fell right off.

Then gradually the town got back to normal as the local men came out of the Forces, but before that happened it seemed to me like a ghost town and my idea of a ghost town is a town full of females.

When Albert was demobbed in 1945 we were faced with a problem. He could have had his old job back but that meant moving to London and we couldn't get anywhere to live there. Also the boys were doing well at school. So we decided to stay where we were. Albert tried to get a job as a milkman but at that time there weren't any going.

When he went to the labour exchange there was the choice of two places. One was with the gas company as a kind of stoker and the other one was a furniture remover. So he went to the furniture removers and they offered him the job. The wages were very low, only five pounds a week which even in 1945 wasn't much. But even at that it was better than it had been. In the old days it was like being a docker. You went into the warehouse and if there was no work you got sent home again without pay. But although the wages were low the work was interesting which I think is important. I mean it's far more important to have low wages and do a job that you really like doing than to have high wages and grind away week after week at something that bores you to tears.

It wasn't static, not sitting on your backside in an office from nine to six. It wasn't even like a milk round where you're going around the same old customers for seven days a week twice a day. You're going everywhere or anywhere. Albert went up to Scotland, into Wales, right down into Cornwall and he was meeting different people all the time. And he learnt about furniture and antiques of all kinds.

Eventually he became a packer because he was such a careful workman and he used to see to the most expensive china – like those Dresden figures that were in all nooks and crannies and worth thousands of pounds. He still got the same money but he looked on it as a sort of promotion. The hours were irregular – when you're moving someone's furniture you can't say, 'I'm knocking off now,' when it comes to five or six o'clock. It can't be left in the street, can it? But we didn't mind irregular hours because we'd been used to them when he was a milkman.

At first I got very worried when he was late coming back at nights. I used to think of all the terrible road accidents that there were and wonder if something of the sort had happened to him. But, as he said, if anything did hit their pantechnicon they wouldn't have suffered I remember one very foggy night, it was ten o'clock and they should have been back at five. I was that worried I rang up the manager of the firm to see if he'd had any news of them.

He said, 'Mrs Powell, I'm worried too. They've got ten thousand pounds' worth of antique furniture on board.'

There's words of comfort for you!

I said, 'To hell with your antiques, I'm thinking about Albert.'

That riled him. 'Well,' he said, 'what do you think I can do? Take a lantern out to look for him? If so, you've got another bloody think coming.'

And he slammed the receiver down. Talk about old-world courtesy.

Albert's had some strange jobs. One place they went to was an old lady's house where she kept twenty-four cats. The council had put a compulsory moving order on her. It was too terrible for words. The place smelt like a sewer. And this old dear was in tears because these cats had got to go to a cats' home. She knew them all individually – she'd lived with them for years. They'd each got their own basket with their name on. Albert and the others hated doing it but if it hadn't been them it would have been someone else.

At another place they were getting a piano up the stairs and halfway it stuck and they couldn't move it up or down. Well the old dear whose piano it was came down with plates of Hovis bread and butter. She said, 'Hovis gives you strength.' Well, I don't know whether it did or not, but when they'd eaten it they gave a mighty heave gouging a great lump out of the wall and the piano went up. The company had an extremely irate letter from the landlord afterwards and they had to repair the damage. But as I said they ought to have passed the letter on to the baker, it was his fault.

Then there was a couple of young men that lived together – they had to move six times. Very charming young men so Albert said, but probably they got so charming around the place that they had to move on. Anyway every single thing in the house was marked with their initials. Except the pots under the bed – they were marked HIS and HERS.

16

THE THREE MONTHS that I spent in hospital – I had two periods of six weeks each – were very different indeed.

I first went because I had a gastric ulcer. It was in 1944 and there was no National Health Service then. I was suffering from indigestion according to my doctor.

I said to him, 'I can't understand why I can't breathe properly.'

But he said it was indigestion and indigestion it had to be till I had a haemorrhage and was rushed into hospital to have a blood transfusion.

I often think that these people who talk about blood and breeding and who have to have blood transfusions don't know what poor old plebeian stuff they've got knocking around in them. I remember when they were giving it to me I said, 'I hope you're giving me blue blood, I'm only used to the best.'

The nursing was splendid but the food and amenities for the patients in the public wards were deplorable. And the lack of privacy most distressing, especially for older people and particularly for those who had gone into hospital for the very first time.

None of the beds had curtains and only in the direst circumstances did they put screens around them. Some of the old people used to complain bitterly about this but it never did them any good because the more they complained the less consideration they got.

I always found during my stay in hospitals, and that includes before and after the National Health Service, that it's best to accept everything that happens to you with the spirit of Job because that's the only way you can really enjoy it. That way you get a reputation for being long suffering and uncomplaining and you're held up to the other patients as a shining light.

The nurses say, 'Look at Mrs Powell, she doesn't ring her bell all day long and she doesn't ask us to keep doing this, that and the other for her.'

The fact that all the other patients get to detest you doesn't matter because they're not looking after you. It's the nurses you've got to rely on for your comfort. So I never complained about anything. I just let it all happen to me.

Once I had recovered sufficiently to be able to walk around the other patients soon forgot their animosity because I did little jobs for them – like getting a jug of water or something out of their locker or bringing them their tea. And then patients are always dying to talk to someone about their home, their husbands and their children. Curiously enough I never found many patients wanted to talk about their operations or what they were in there for. Not then.

When they get home they do, but I think it's too near to them in hospital. They try to pretend almost that it doesn't exist. It's rather like a conversation I once overheard between two women.

One was saying to the other, 'Oh, I've got such pains in my stomach and I have to keep on taking these Rennies to relieve it.'

So the other said, 'Haven't you been to the doctor, then?'

She said, 'No. I'm scared to go to the doctor because he might send me to the hospital and they might say it's cancer.'

Well, the pain wouldn't go away would it? But she thought that if she didn't give it a name, it wasn't there. And that's how I found they were in hospital.

Although as I've said I kept quiet, before the National Health Act there was plenty to complain about in the public wards.

The meals were the worst thing. They used to be served on battered old tin trays with no cloth on of course, and as I was in there with ulcers it was mainly cod that tasted and felt like cottonwool. And the mashed potatoes had hard concrete lumps in them and were nearly always stone cold. You really had to be hungry to eat it. Mostly the sweet was a milk pudding and it was either so stiff you could have bounced it on the floor, or it was hard grains floating around in milk.

And when it was time for the bedpans the nurses used to

deal them out on beds as you would a pack of cards. And there we used to sit parked on them, in full view of each other, and there was one toilet roll between four. And we'd throw it from bed to bed and sometimes we'd miss and it would roll down the ward like a large streamer. And we'd go into hysterics of mirth. It was the only way to accept the humiliation of it all.

That was my first stay in hospital and I hoped it would be my last.

But some years after, by this time there was the National Health Service, I discovered that I had a lump about the size of a small marble underneath my breast. I went straight to the doctor and he sent me to the hospital for an examination.

And what a change I found. You were treated as though you mattered. Even the waiting-room was different. No dark green paint, whitewash, and wooden benches. There were separate chairs with modern magazines – not the kind that Noah had around in the Ark.

They told me that I should have to have a minor operation for the cyst to be removed, but that I would only be in there about a week.

And again what a difference I saw. The beds for instance. The bed that I'd had before was like lying on the pebbles on Brighton beach. I got to know every lump in it and used to arrange myself around them. But now I had a rubber mattress. I felt as though I could have lain there for ever.

And the food was beautiful. All served on brightly coloured trays with the right cutlery. I remember one day I was waiting for my lunch when the matron came round; she saw my tray and said to the nurse, 'Isn't this patient having fish for her lunch today?'

And the nurse said, 'Yes, Matron, she is.'

'Well why hasn't she got a fish knife and fork then? Change it instantly.'

I was amazed. I couldn't have cared less because we hadn't got any fish knives and forks at home. But that just shows you, doesn't it?

And there was variety. I don't think we ever saw the same meal twice in one week and that needs some doing. It just showed what kind of kitchen staff they'd got. Presumably under the National Health Act they could afford to pay them more wages than before. When I was in service you were considered the lowest of the low if you worked in hospital kitchens.

And every bed had got curtains and they were drawn not only at bedpan time but at any time you were attended to.

There was only one thing that was exactly the same and I suppose always will be and that is that neither nurses, house surgeons nor the visiting specialists would ever answer any questions about your condition. In fact they never stayed long enough by your bed for you to get the question out.

I think that a generation that's brought up on *Emergency Ward 10* and *Dr Kildare* must suffer great disillusionment when they go into hospital. In all the time I've spent there no doctor or house surgeon has ever sat on my bed talking to me about my complaint.

As for the specialists they don't even look at you. They seem to stare right over your head. They frighten you to death. They stand there looking so stern you feel you've got every ailment under the sun and you're not likely to last much longer and they're weighing up who's coming into your bed when you've gone.

And the nurses seem to think that along with physical deterioration goes mental deterioration. You get these young nurses saying, 'Come along, Mother, be a good girl. Put your nightie on and pop into bed.' As though you were suffering from senile decay and didn't understand plain English. It riled me the way they did that. I hate being jollied along at any time, let alone when in hospital.

As I said, I went into this hospital to have this cyst removed from my breast and the night before the operation the Sister stuck a form under my nose for me to sign. I hate forms at the best of times and when I'd recovered from the shock I read it and discovered that I'd got to agree that in the event of them discovering that I needed major surgery I was prepared to have it done. At once I knew that they were going to slash my breast off otherwise why go into all this palaver if it was just a cyst.

So I signed – and I knew what it meant.

I wasn't shocked when I came to after the operation and found I was bandaged up in miles of bandages. I knew it hadn't been just a cyst.

I asked the nurse of course but she just said, 'Go to sleep, Mother.'

But Mother knew. The nurse wouldn't tell me because she felt I was going to suffer from the shock. But I'd suffered from the shock the night before when I read that form.

About a couple of days after the operation the house surgeon told me that they had found a tumour there and had to remove the breast, but that it was a non-malignant one and I would be going home shortly. It didn't take me long to get over the operation and I was soon able to get up and help a bit.

We had some lively people in that ward. There was an unfortunate woman there who used to suffer with the most rude noises. She couldn't help it. But when she let one go the patients would call out, 'There's a bomb just gone off, Nurse,' and then a little later, 'It's all right, the all clear's gone now.'

There was another woman. She was only in there to have her bunions done. She was a card if ever there was one.

She said to me, 'This is the first time I've had a bed to myself for forty years.'

So I said, 'Is it? It must be awful being separated after all those years.'

'It isn't,' she said. 'It's bloody marvellous. Sharing a bed with my old man is nothing but sweat and swill.'

She said she wasn't going back to sharing a bed, which shows that hospital life has a lot to answer for.

Some of the patients looked at me a bit queerly. They told me later that they thought I'd have delayed reaction emotion about losing my breast. But strangely enough I wasn't ever really upset.

My mother was more. She kept weeping like mad by my bedside. But if you're a young girl and you're hoping to get married it's a far more serious thing, isn't it? You'd have to tell your young man and explaining it away would be a bit embarrassing. But I'd got a husband who I knew wouldn't think any the worse of me because of it. And when they told me it was non-malignant I was quite happy about it. Naturally I would have preferred to have kept it. It wasn't the kind of thing that I could chuck off and not know I hadn't got. It's not the kind of an appendage that doesn't matter whether you have it or not. It's not like your appendix. But no, I wasn't too upset about it.

Then three days before I was to go home they came up to me again, put the curtains round the bed and I prepared myself for another shock.

In came the Sister this time. I'd always thought of her as a bit of a martinet. Mind you, you need a Sister that's a martinet because the other hospital I was in the Sister was very strict indeed and I used to feel sorry for the nurses, but we realized when she went on holiday what a difference a strict Sister made to our lives because once she was out of the way the nurses didn't care a bit. They used to laugh and joke and make the most terrible row and we never got half the attention that we had when she was there. But this one I'd thought was a hard woman – unfeeling – but what a change. She was kindness itself to me. She sat there by my bed for half an hour. She told me that they'd got a report back from the Marie Curie hospital in Hampstead that my growth was malignant and that I'd got to go there and have radium treatment.

It was only then that I really thought about cancer. As soon as she mentioned the Marie Curie I knew what the hospital was for so I knew I'd got cancer and I was very upset then for the rest of that day. I know I wept a few times to myself and that. The thing I asked Sister to do for me was to catch my mother before she came in to visit me and tell her because I didn't feel as though I could. I knew she'd be terribly upset about it, which she was.

But strangely enough by next morning I'd recovered. I thought – oh, well, here goes. Lots of people go to the Marie Curie and they don't all die. I mean if you've got to have cancer you couldn't have it in a better place than in the breast because once you've had it removed most of it's gone.

So by the next day I'd got over it and as I wasn't due to go for a week I asked if I could go home. 'No,' came the answer. They wouldn't let me go because they were frightened I wouldn't come back. But after a day or two I got lively and me and this woman with bunions kicked up such a shindy larking around that Sister said, 'All right, you've won, you can go home for the weekend but don't forget to come back.' Of course, I would come back in any case.

When I got to this Marie Curie hospital in Hampstead I found there were many far worse than me because they'd let it go such a long time before they'd been to a doctor, and it had spread and gone into an arm as well. So really and truly it really does pay to see a doctor in the very early stages because it never affected me in that way.

I used to go every day for radium treatment – just five minutes a day. It was in a little room that there was this sort of Heath Robinson contraption that hovers over you. You have to lie down and there's a door about a foot thick, which is closed on you and of course I suffer appallingly from claustrophobia. I didn't mind the radium treatment but the thought of being shut in that room was almost too much for me. But the nurses were very good. There was a little glass window and they'd look at me. But although it was only five minutes it seemed like half an hour and I'd imagine they'd forgotten the time.

Anyway I had six weeks of that treatment and then I went home. I had to go back once a month for the first three months and then once every three months and then once a year. I still do now although it was over ten years ago and I've never had a recurrence.

When I got back came the problem of a bra. The old bras I'd got were no good at all. The Marie Curie had given me the address of where to go for one on the National Health Service. Maybe now it's a better model but at that time, believe me, it was pure stodge. An appalling pink-coloured thing, a cross between a liberty bodice and a strait jacket. I've never seen anything like it in my life. I thought they would have tried to do something better than that. I mean just at a time when you feel mutilated and even though you try to laugh about it, you do feel mutilated, you'd have thought they'd have produced something artistic.

Well I accepted it because it was on the National Health but I didn't wear it. I bought myself a pair of falsies and a bra to go with them. I only needed one falsie, but they wouldn't sell them singly. There's a waste of money. It was the cult of the huge bra à la Jane Russell and breasts was all coming in then and everybody was endeavouring to look twice the size they really were. So perhaps it was as well I didn't get them singly otherwise I'd have looked unbalanced.

Of course wearing a falsie can be a very tricky thing. The first time I put a bathing costume on and went swimming I was very disconcerted to see it bobbing merrily around on top of the waves. I hastily stuffed it back but I felt awful. I don't know whether anyone noticed or not but it was a pale pink colour and it looked most peculiar. Anyway after that I used cottonwool. I thought of buying one of those bras that you blow up and you're provided with a little pump. I would only have blown up one side but then I thought it would be a bit awkward if I had a puncture. I couldn't really carry a repair outfit around with me, could I? So I gave up that idea.

But though I joked about it then and joke about it now, losing a breast does something to you in a sort of psychological way. You never feel the same person again. Not to yourself. Maybe you seem the same to other people. In the beginning you feel degraded and then you don't feel a complete woman any more. All right there's things on the market to make you look the same externally but there's nothing on the market that makes you feel the same internally.

But don't let me make a big thing out of this psychological feeling. What I would say to anyone would be if they suspect anything like that is to go straight away to a doctor. Mine was only a breast operation – one amongst many, but I made a friend at the Marie Curie who was there for an internal cancer operation – and a very big operation indeed. She was in hospital for months, but now she's out, she's doing a full-time job in domestic service and she still only has to go in once a year like me. She caught it in what were the early stages and although the operation was a big one because it was internal it hasn't spread all over her body. But I had a sister-in-law who suffered the pains and wouldn't go in and when she had to it was far too late. If it's caught early mostly it can be cured and even if you have to have the operation I had you can still live a very happy life.

17

SOME PEOPLE JOIN evening classes because they're bored and want company. I didn't. I just wanted to be able to converse with my sons. I found that I wasn't able to do this because they'd all won scholarships and gone to the grammar school. There they were, eleven and thirteen and fifteen, sitting at the table talking among themselves and Albert and I were completely left out. It didn't worry Albert – he didn't care whether he conversed or not. He likes to be quiet but I enjoy making conversation and I hated being excluded from it.

You hear children say that they've got nothing in common with their parents and the psychiatrists tell you that parents mustn't become divorced from their children, that they must make efforts to understand them. They say you don't understand them because if you never talk to them you can't understand them. As well as cooking, washing and doing the cleaning for them you've got to be able to talk to them otherwise they consider you less than the dust. They won't realize that you've worked so darned hard looking after them that you're tired. Oh no, if you're not bothering to keep your old brains exercised then there's something wrong with you. There's nothing wrong with them if they don't understand these things.

Anyway I found that conversation was reduced to the weather and the headlines in the newspapers and after you'd said that there was nothing else to say. Then I read an article that said that the more one soaks up knowledge the more the brain expands to absorb it. Something like Parkinson's Law where the work expands so as to fill the time available for its completion, which is the truest law I've ever known. You've only got to look at our town council's employees. They demonstrate Parkinson's Law to a tee. So I decided that although I'd never believed in keeping up with the Joneses, I'd try and keep up with the boys – and that to do this I'd got to start educating myself by going to evening classes. I thought, well, I'll try this theory out.

It didn't work with me this Parkinson's Law – maybe because I started too late. I thought, oh, well, the more you take on the more your brain expands – and I took on three things straight away – French, social science, and something called metaphysical philosophy. This last one I took as a sort of status symbol. The very name of it! I imagined myself surprising all my sons with some gem of intellectual conversation that I'd got through this metaphysical philosophy. A sort of female Oscar Wilde I visualized myself as, with repartee and wit flashing round the table. But after six weeks of classes I hadn't understood a word of metaphysical philosophy. The dictionary defined it as abstruse and abstract and, believe me, the dictionary definition was correct. Certainly it was abstruse.

We had to do homework on it and we were picked at random to get up in class and explain in layman's terms what we'd written. Well, I copied mine clear out of the book. I hadn't any idea what it meant. I was just hoping that I'd get away with it. Unfortunately I was picked one night to get up and I couldn't say that I'd copied it out of the book. It would have been too terrible for words, especially when you want to be a big noise and I always liked to be the big noise. So I stumbled through it somehow or other and the teacher said, 'I don't really think you've grasped what it means yet.' I thought – no, you and me both because even if you've grasped what it means you can't explain it in lay terms. So after six weeks I gave it up. I didn't bother about metaphysical philosophy any more. But I did keep on with the French and social science.

Social science I thought would have some bearing on life; the social approach, not history with dates and figures or what's been. I thought it would enable me to co-relate the sort of life I was leading to the world around and would give me an idea of what made people tick – that kind of thing. It didn't, but that's what I thought it would do.

I suppose I started where most people were leaving off. There must have been a lot that I should have studied before I even took on social science but I didn't know. People used to say, why didn't I take up a craft, but I didn't want to do things with my hands – tatting, lampshade-making, glove-making and things like that. I'd quite enough to do with my hands running a home and I didn't want to start threading beads or petit point or making pictures out of bits of felt. That sort of thing's all very well if you've got an artistic sense, but I haven't. I'm devoid of it. No – I wanted to use my brains; I wanted to be able to talk to my boys. I wanted to be able to baffle them with social science, then we could sit at the table and have unintelligible conversations, all of us, because as soon as there was a gap in what they said I could rush in with mine, and they wouldn't be able to understand me any more than I could understand them.

The French course was ludicrous. In my imagination I thought that as they were learning French they would help me. I didn't realize that the rot had set in with regards to children and their parents. My generation had revered their parents; whatever their parents said was law and gospel and you believed what they said and you gave them respect as well as love. But by the time I became a parent children no longer thought that what their parents said was true or gave them any respect at all. When I used to come out with my little *bons mots* in French they hooted with laughter at my pronunciation. I pronounced the words as they looked. I got old Hugo's French dictionary out at the table and I'd say, '*Voulez vous passer le sel s'il vous plaît*,' saying it like you see it in print.

And they'd say, 'Mum wants the vinegar? Pepper, Mum? Pass Mum the mustard, Dad.'

The little blighters knew I meant pass the salt but they purposely misunderstood.

When I said, 'Chacun à son goût,' they'd say, 'Get up, Dad, you're sitting in something. You've got your arse in the goo.' They just made fun of me all the time. But I plodded on. Once I start anything I do it till the bitter end, except for metaphysical philosophy.

The teachers, too, vary in their approach. I've had ever so many kinds of teachers. Some of them have the idea of ramming a lot of facts and figures down you – perhaps it's because they were taught that way themselves and they haven't been able to get out of it, but students who go voluntarily want the lessons made interesting. They naturally find facts and figures unpalatable and that's why I think attendances fall off. Some teachers don't make allowance for the fact that all we go there for is leisure-time activities, that we haven't had much schooling and that we require time to assimilate knowledge. They get impatient. And you have only got to make people who are a bit insecure about their early education feel that they don't know enough for them not to come any more. They're very vulnerable. You're vulnerable with your children but at least you can laugh it off. It may hurt you – it got beneath my skin even in my own home. But in classes if you have a teacher who makes you feel that you're ignorant, you think well what the bloody hell am I doing here? You haven't gone there to be humiliated so you stay away. Not all teachers are like that. Some are very good indeed. But still you can sense that some are thinking to themselves, she couldn't understand this when she was young so what hopes has she of understanding it now?

We students know that teachers are often tired. That they've been teaching all day and that this is only an extra to them because they want to earn a bit more money. The advantage is that with us at any rate at the beginning everybody is very enthusiastic. They want to learn. And yet again it's funny because in any class where you have to use your brain attendances keep dropping. You may start with about thirty and you're lucky to have got ten by the time the course is over.

1 don't know about the handicraft courses. I only attended one. It was flower-arranging and that was a lark if ever there was one; it was an absolute riot. The teacher must have had a marvellously aesthetic eye because she could make the most wonderful arrangements out of next to nothing, from the most unlikely materials.

She set us a task one week. She gave each of us a list of things that we had to make an arrangement with; my list said two or three smooth round pebbles, a piece of driftwood, a cabbage leaf and a stick of celery. I thought to myself: this is me, it's right up my street. I got the stones and the driftwood down on the beach and it didn't take me long to get a couple of sticks of celery and a cabbage leaf. First I tried arranging it on a flat dish among some wire mesh in a sort of – well it was a kind of . . . I thought it was a . . . but it wasn't, so I took it all out and I got a lump of plasticine and started again. I stuck the stones round it and the cabbage leaf (wilting) and the two sticks of celery (brown at the ends). You ought to have seen the result. I carted it up there just for a laugh. Everybody had got their arrangements,

169

some had very fine muslin cloth draped over them, some in cardboard boxes and all were very lovely – even I could see that. And I came up with mine in an old brown carrier bag.

So they said to me, 'Where's your arrangement?'

I said, 'In this bag.'

'In a bag,' they said. 'Well, what is it?'

'Well,' I said, 'it's a cabbage leaf and two sticks of celery and pebbles.'

When I got it out everybody nearly died of laughter. They made ever such rude remarks. So they lost one pupil at handicrafts.

It was when I was fifty-seven that I decided that I would study in real earnest, not just as a leisure-time activity but where I really sat for something. Mind you, I'd been in earnest about the other things. I'd enjoyed them, had a lot of fun, made a lot of friends, and acquired a lot of knowledge. But I thought I'd like to do something in competition with the younger ones. So I went to the technical college.

I found joining the class there a far different proposition from joining the leisure-time activities. In the leisure-time activities most of the people were about my age because we were doing things because we'd retired or because our families had grown up. But studying for 'O' level were young people who for some reason or other had failed when they were fifteen and were trying again. So when I tried to sign on I thought I might be rejected on account of my age.

I waited for hours in the queue; on the signing-on days there are queues everywhere. You'd think that half the town was dying to go to learn. So I waited in the queue and when I finally reached the young man who was behind the desk he looked at me in amazement.

He said, 'What are you doing here, this isn't a leisure-time activity, you know? This is studying leading to an examination.'

'I know that,' I said.

So he said, 'Well, you obviously don't want to do that. You're in the wrong place.'

I said, 'I know what I'm doing. Is there any reason why I can't take "O" level English literature?'

That and the way I said it put him back on his heels. 'So he said, 'Well, no, I suppose there isn't really.'

Anyway I finally convinced him I was serious. But he wouldn't sign me on.

He said, 'I think you'd better go and see the principal.'

I don't know why. So I had to join another queue. Anyway when I finally got to the principal he also looked astonished.

He said, 'You know this is a two-year course at least. It could be three if you don't pass it in two years. Are you prepared to do all that? It's not much good starting and then leaving because you might be taking somebody else's place.'

That was all a load of my eye and Betty Martin, believe me. By the time the first year ended there was room for another half as many again. I made what I thought were keen noises.

'Oh,well,' he said, 'I suppose it's all right,' in a very half-hearted manner.

He thought it was a waste of his time and my time.

Mind you, he was quite right. He's not there for bene-volent reasons. He's there to see that young people who haven't got an education get one. And I didn't blame him in the least. Why should he bother about the older people? It was up to the older people to be very self-assertive for themselves and I certainly was.

Anyway I joined the original queue again. I was in queues about two hours that night. Finally I got up to the young man again.

'Oh, it's you is it,' he said.

So I said, 'He says it's all right.'

'Oh, well,' he said, 'then it must be. Anyway you'll be glad to know there's another old lady in the class apart from you.'

When I got to the class I found the other old lady was around forty so it was really very flattering. I thought that either she was a lot older than she said or I was a lot younger-looking. Still, contrary to all scepticism, I was in.

The class started off about thirty strong. Some took their exam in a year because they'd only just failed before they left school and all they needed was a bit of brushing up. I think it's stupid that when you've failed an examination they don't tell you what particular thing you failed in – whether it was grammar, the essay, the dictation, the spelling, or what. It's left to you to realize for yourself. So you don't know what you should be swotting. I felt sorry for the youngsters, they were so confused. But some of the class took the exam after a year and as they never came back I assumed that they had passed. My guess had been quite right: the class started off with thirty but it had dropped right down to fourteen and by the end of the second year there were only ten of us left to take the exam. I suppose it got boring for some of the young ones. There was so much else in life, so much else they could be doing. And it's not just the evenings that are taken up. You've got to study at home. As well as the homework that you're set, you're expected to read books. So inevitably people did drop out. It wasn't the quality of the teacher – we had a fine teacher. And as I hoped I would, I enjoyed being with and working with young people. They were great fun.

I felt embarrassed at first – especially the first night. I got there about a quarter of an hour before the class started, thinking I might be able to walk into a more or less empty room and that the others would come in gradually and I wouldn't have to meet them all *en masse* so to speak. But when I got there the class was nearly full up and what made it doubly embarrassing was that they thought I was the teacher. It was terrible. They jumped up when I went in and came forward, said who they were and asked me what my name was. Then I realized what they thought.

I said, 'I'm not the teacher.'

'Not the teacher,' they said. 'Well, then you're in the wrong class.'

'No, I'm not,' I said. 'This is English "O" level, isn't it? The first year of English "O" level?'

They said, 'Yes.'

'Well, I'm one of the students.'

And they all laughed, though I must admit in a very nice way.

There were more girls than boys in the class, but apart from this woman of forty I could have been grandmother to any of them. It wasn't long before I was left in splendid isolation because the forty-year-old soon dropped out. Apparently she'd gone into it because although she was married, her children were off her hands and she'd taken up working in an office again. This entailed a lot of letter writing and she wanted to get her grammar right, but she reckoned this course didn't really do anything for her. I think it would have if she'd stayed.

But the young ones were fun and I never once had any embarrassment. The fact was that they were there because they were keen on being educated and getting on. They weren't a lot of hooligans or layabouts.

Two years later when I went to take the exam I got a terrible shock. It was held in a church hall and I thought there'd just be me and the nine youngsters who were left in the class. When I got there, there were about ninety-nine youngsters from other places – and me looking like Mrs Methuselah. I managed to find my own nine that I'd gone through with and I stuck to them like a leech. I didn't want to feel out of it. We stood around with everybody saying that they knew they were going to fail. You have to say that before because it sort of lets you down lightly if you do fail.

Eventually we filed into the hall. It was all very austere and frightening. Every desk at a certain distance from the next, and you're not allowed to touch anything till you're given the word to go. Then they come round with the list of questions and when you look at it you nearly die. Your mind is a complete blank and you're sure that you're never going to be able to answer any of them. Then you sort of pull yourself together and things become a bit clearer and you think well I've got three hours. Three hours seems a long time at first but the trouble is to keep writing. Your hand aches; during the last hour my hand ached so much I thought I'd never be able to keep going. Then I glanced around at this sea of earnest young faces and I couldn't help wondering what all these young people were going to do if they passed. How intent they seemed on striving to go one better. And I thought of what my life might have been like if I'd been able to take up the scholarship that I'd won when I was thirteen. And then I thought, well maybe it would have been like the verger in that Somerset Maugham short story.

He'd been a verger for years and he couldn't read or write and it hadn't mattered. But a new vicar took over and found that he was illiterate. So he was sacked. He was wandering around disconsolate and he saw a tobacconist shop for sale. He bought it and he did so well that he ended up with a chain of shops. One day he went to the bank and the manager said, 'Why don't you invest your money?' And handed him a prospectus.

So he said, 'It's no good showing me this, I can't read.'

The manager said, 'Can't read and you've done so well? Imagine where you would have got if you could have read.'

And the man said, 'Well, if I could have read I would still have been a verger.'

So I often think if I could have taken up the scholarship

and become a teacher, as was my ambition, life might not have been nearly so interesting as it has been.

Anyway even though I allowed my thoughts to wander I managed to get through the paper. I couldn't answer all the questions, simply because the time limit beat me. I suppose when you're younger your mind is more agile and certainly your hands are.

When we came out we all got together and had a celebration, coffee and cream cakes, the school tuckshop sort of thing. Then we all said how badly we'd done, once again preparing the way in case we'd failed. We all said we knew we hadn't passed and yet we were very cheerful about it. But when we got the results we had all passed.

This success spurred me on. I thought: well I've got 'O' level so why not have a go at 'A' level. Mind you the 'A' level was a very different proposition from 'O' level. There was Shakespeare, Tennyson, and Huxley and books like that to be read and *I, Claudius* by Robert Graves. I thought I'd never get through it, what with everybody getting murdered and what not all the way through the book. Then just after we had started we were told that we'd have to complete the course in a year instead of two years. This was because the numbers were so low that if we didn't the class would have to close. This I felt was asking a lot – and it might be expensive because the examination fees were quite high.

But I'm glad I took the chance. We had a marvellous teacher, I've got to hand it to him. Anyone who couldn't assimilate the knowledge that he dished out and couldn't understand the books when he explained them should have stayed at home and done fretwork or tatting. He was wonderful, but all too fast the examination day came round. It was the church hall again. This time when I got there, there was a bottle of smelling salts and a bottle of eau-de-Cologne on my desk with a card saying 'Good luck, Gran' – was my face red? I asked the others afterwards who put them there but none of them would admit to it. They were another grand set of youngsters.

Well, as you must have gathered, I passed. Once again success went to my head. So now I'm studying for my 'A' level in history. I've done one year and have got one more year to do and I hope to pass that as well. After that who knows? Has anyone ever got a university scholarship at the age of sixty-five?

People ask me what value has it been to you? What have you got out of it? This kind of remark sends me screaming up the wall. It's as though you're expected to show them money – or some object that you've been able to buy because you've acquired some knowledge. I suppose it's the sort of bloody ignorance you've got to expect in a materialistic world.

I'll tell you what I've got out of it. I've increased my fluency of self-expression both in the spoken and written word. I've got a new confidence. I've found beauty that I didn't know existed in the English language – and you tell me where you can buy beauty.

Studying for the 'A' levels has given me an insight into books that I hadn't got before. I never did read rubbish but when you come to books by people like Shakespeare and Tennyson and the teacher opens your eyes for you, it's like Ali Baba and the treasure cave. I'd never liked poetry because I hadn't been able to make head or tail of what the poet was getting at. But when you have a teacher whose whole being radiates as he talks about it, who so obviously loves it, who wants you to love it too and who takes the trouble to explain it to you, a new life opens for you. So even if you only get more pleasure out of reading it's worthwhile.

Who wants money when you've got public libraries? Your life can be very rich when you have these so rich in knowledge and beauty. And this is what that teacher gave me: not just knowledge but the desire for and the direction to go to acquire more. And any man who can do that for people has reached the peak of human achievement. Well, that's what I think anyway.

18

BEFORE I STARTED studying history for my 'A' level at the ripe age of sixty-one you could have written all that I knew about history on a single page. And that all boils down to the way I was taught at my elementary school. We weren't taught that history was a record of the living past but that it was a record of a dead one. Nothing was presented as the vivid pageant of the times or the fascinating study of the people who'd lived in those times. It was nothing but a collection of facts, figures, and dates.

When I left school all I really knew of history was that King Alfred burned the cakes, King Harold got shot in the eye, and King Richard had a humpback. What a heritage to leave school with. Another bad thing about school in those days was that you never left with a desire to learn more, which surely is the whole reason for education – that you leave with a desire to learn more and that you know how and where to find knowledge. Mind you, you left school knowing the three Rs which is more than many do today.

But looking back I can't really blame the teachers because the same teacher had to teach every subject; not like now when you have specialist teachers for each subject.

Since I've been studying history I've listened far more attentively to my mother's tales about Victorian life – she was born in 1880. Before I never used to take much notice of her. I used to let her drone on.

She says – and it's true – that people think that life for the poor is as hard now as it was many years ago. I must confess I used to think the same. She tells me about her grandparents. Both of them had to go to the workhouse when they were old because the Government gave no money, they only provided workhouses. And none of their children could afford to keep them so they just had to go there.

My mother's grandmother died in one and because of one. She was over sixty and you might say she died of old age, but the conditions there accelerated it. My mother's grandfather lived on, though he couldn't walk, and when his sons used to go and see him he'd cry and say to them, 'Oh, get a cart, get a wheelbarrow, get anything – only get me out of this terrible place.'

Eventually my mother's father did get him out and took him home. And the old man used to tell my mother the most harrowing tales. What an appalling place it was.

It was a workhouse and an asylum all in one. The laundry used to be done down in the cellars and the reek of that yellow soap and decaying bodies was always with them. The sick and the infirm just lay in the wards with no one to look after them – only the other inmates, if they felt like it.

When it got dark there was just one oil lamp for everyone and they had nothing to do but just sit and gaze at each other. Most of them were illiterate so they couldn't help themselves.

Things like this don't happen now. It's history. But it's history within living memory and it's history which accounts for the way some people think and behave today.

When my mother was a girl, the workhouse was at the end of their garden and the children from there used to go to the same school. They used to be known as the workhouse brats, with their grey woollen dresses in the winter and grey cotton dresses in the summer. In the area where Mum lived whole families used to go into the workhouse in the winter and in the summer when there was more work about they'd come out again. But while they were in they would be separated, the women from the husbands and the children from both. The shadow of the workhouse hung over every working-class family.

My mother went into domestic service in 1895. The people she worked for had acquired their wealth in trade as so many middle-class people had at that time. They had sold their town house and bought a big one in the country, filling it with the latest in Victoriana.

She got ten pounds a year there, paid quarterly as it was too small an amount to be paid oftener. Out of this she had to buy herself one new dress a year. She wore the same dresses summer and winter. But then of course you couldn't buy anything ready-made. She's told me it took seven yards of serge material and seven yards of lining and of course not only did she have to buy the material, she had to pay to have it made as well. So she had very little money left out of her ten pounds.

In this particular job, the under-servants were expected when they went out to wear a black bonnet provided by the employers. Mother simply hated wearing this bonnet. She was always a bit on the militant side. To her that bonnet was a sign of servitude and she thought it should be resisted. So one day she went out in her own hat and she was seen from the drawing-room. When she came in she was called for and she got a severe telling off. She didn't dare do it again but she looked for and got another job.

At the next place she got twelve pounds a year, paid monthly, with a Lord Jisson, VC. He lived outside Chichester at a place called Bosham. It was a much larger grander place, and he kept a pack of hounds. But it was run on military lines and everybody's task was allotted to them. There was a housekeeper there who kept tabs on the women and a butler who kept tabs on the menservants, and for everyone a list of duties was laid down. Whereas in the other places she was at the beck and call of all and sundry, here she had to stick rigorously to the duties. And the housekeeper saw to the standing orders.

All the servants had beer supplied twice a day, even the under-servants. Mother didn't drink hers, she used to save it for the organ-grinder. Apparently an organ-grinder used to come twice a week with his monkey and this monkey had developed a taste for beer. So the organ-grinder used to drink what he could and give the rest to the monkey.

After which, Mother said, that monkey used to cut the most unusual capers and this would be a talking point and an enjoyment for the servants for days.

Of course today it sounds trite and shows a lack of education. But those were the kind of events that you had to look forward to. Some form of variety to relieve from the humdrum. You had no education and little hope of advancement in position or in money, and no security at all of course.

As for the advanced education, that was still a pipe-dream. And it wasn't until the poor did get an advanced education that they were able to speak up for themselves, that they became, as you might say, powerful advocates for their own class. Left to the upper class nothing was going to be done. Why should they kill the goose that laid their golden eggs.

But things were improving even then, compared to my grandmother's days, because when my grandmother was in service there was a sort of feudal system.

She worked in a large manor house and the man who owned it owned the entire village; all the land for miles around and every cottage were owned by him too and he was very particular indeed about how they were kept. Nobody from outside could come and live in his village. He made sure that nothing and nobody changed. As Grandmother said, this system had its advantages because when the villagers were ill, medicines and food were sent down from the big house. But, she said, even so the villagers weren't grateful. They used to detest having to doff their caps to the squire who they felt was rude and arrogant to them. Still Grandmother reckoned that the villagers then had a better life than when things became freer for the working class. Because then nobody really cared at all.

This was always a point of disagreement between my mother and grandmother. Mother was a stickler for her rights, not women's rights but her rights, and as far as she could she fought for them. Of course she couldn't break the system, but occasionally she bent it.

One thing she couldn't bend however was the business of waking up in the morning. It always had been a servant's nightmare. At one place, though, she came to a good arrangement with one of the gardeners. Every night she would tie a piece of string to her big toe and throw the string out of the window. When the gardener used to come round at five o'clock in the morning he'd give it a mighty yank and so wake Mother up. Apparently she was never late, though on more than one occasion she hobbled round her work for the rest of the day.

The saying 'early to bed and early to rise makes a man healthy, wealthy, and wise' I've always thought a stupid one. Yet there must be something in it since at any rate for much of our lives my mother, Albert and I have had to get up very early. It hasn't made us wealthy or necessarily wise but we've certainly been healthy. Albert and I are both now drawing the old-age pension. So I suppose that proves something.

19

WHEN I SEE the words Retirement and Old Age I ask myself why are the two coupled together? Why does retirement suddenly and automatically mean old age? Retirement shouldn't make a radical change in life. But it does, especially for men. When they retire their life changes completely but a woman's doesn't because she still goes on doing more or less the same things, particularly if she's a woman who hasn't gone out to work. She still does the housework, the shopping, the cooking, and the laundry.

Before a man retires he should start thinking what it's going to mean. But he doesn't so when the time comes the conditions take him unawares and he's not able to adapt himself to them. What he often mistakenly thinks is that when he retires it's going to be a marvellous existence. All the things he's not had time to do when he was working he's going to be able to do then. Perhaps he's got a hobby. Perhaps he likes to make things at home or collect things or look after the garden. But what he doesn't realize is that these things that fitted in nicely in his spare time are nothing like sufficient as full-time occupations.

I think men become so apathetic and that's why life seems to hold so much less happiness for them in retirement than it does for a woman. I'm going by the old people where I live and where my mother lives. I do quite a bit for them and there's hardly any men left there now. Amongst all the families, in about forty houses, there can't be more than six men. And it's not because the women were so much younger than the men, it's just that the men didn't adapt themselves to a life of leisure, didn't know what to do with themselves and so like the old soldiers in the song they just faded away. Men are not as resourceful as women, nor do they adapt to new circumstances.

A man leaves school, he gets his job and he plods along till he's sixty, sixty-five, or seventy and when work ends he doesn't know what to do with himself. He feels he's got no place; he's in limbo. The wife doesn't want him at home. She loves her husband, of course she does, but she loves him to go off to work at eight or nine in the morning and come home at five or six at night. She doesn't want him under her feet all day long. She likes her life, a life whereby he's not in the home all day and she can go out and visit her cronies and do her shopping. All of a sudden he wants to join in with these things, he wants to go shopping with her; he wants to know where she's been and what she's been talking about, and very soon acrimonious discussions start between people who have lived as Darby and Joan all their lives. It's only because the man doesn't think and doesn't try to make a place for himself in the world of retirement. Mind you, the wife can help. Together they can plan his life – make some sort of timetable. They don't have to stick to it religiously but it will give them something to go by until the man has worked out a definite way of life for himself.

I often think it's a great pity that a man can't retire gradually, doing half a day for a time while he sorts himself out. The trouble is he believes that all the week life will be just like it was at weekends. And while he's enjoyed his weekends when he was working all the week, he hasn't realized that it's because he's working that he enjoyed them. He doesn't understand that it was the change he enjoyed and that there's no longer going to be any change.

Another thing, most councils like ours run courses on retirement but they don't get the people they should. They don't get the working-class person, the man who has done a physical job and is going to find it harder to use time than a person whose work has employed his brain. A man who does a hard physical job all week doesn't come home at night and pick up a book and read, he probably just turns the telly on. He doesn't think about using his brains. He probably thinks he hasn't got any. I've heard many old men say, 'Oh no, I've never done anything like that and I'm too old to start now.' But they're not too old. It's the middle class who go to these courses but the others need them even more. And the things that you can learn to do now! Every occupation, every hobby is covered so you don't have to be intellectual if you don't want to. This is something to think about and to do that will make for a happy life in retirement.

But no, these men don't. Then I hear them say they've got time to go and visit their children, and see more of them. They don't realize that their children have got a life of their own by now, a life in which their parents have not played a part before; and you can't expect them and their families automatically to alter their way of life because you have leisure time on your hands. Married children have got their own work and their own friends and they haven't much place for you in their life and there's no reason why they should have, because if they're relying on the companionship of their aged parents, their own lives must be very barren, indeed. But the parents won't realize this. They get disgruntled and say, 'Ah, there you are. You get old and even your own children don't want you. You might as well be on the scrap heap.'

I don't see why you should expect your children to devote their lives to you. When your family get married you've given them up. You've done your duty in life. You've brought them into the world, you've fed them, clothed them and educated them to the best of your ability. Let them lead their own lives, I say. Don't make them feel that their mother and father are sitting stewing over in their minds about what they do or don't do for them. Everybody should be complete in themselves and you shouldn't have to rely on other people to provide a purpose or to make you feel that you're important in life.

I think nowadays that old people are lucky. There's never been so much done and thought about for them as there is today, but they must help as well.

Those I feel really sorry for are the ones who live on their own and who have no one to visit them or care for them. Perhaps they've driven people away by their cantankerousness but to be old, poor, and cantankerous is the last word in a lonely existence.

Another sad thing to see is those people who've lived in council houses and who have to move to a small flat. You can't blame the council because they've got a long waiting list of young people with families who need houses. Obviously it's only right that one or perhaps two people living in a three-bedroomed house should move out but they're taken away from everyone that they know. Some of the council flats for old people in Brighton for instance are sited in a road where they are isolated. No one goes up that road unless they live there or unless they have to deliver there. So sometimes from morning to night the old people, particularly those who can't get out, never see anything of life at all. It's a terrible existence for them, a kind of apartheid. Then they start to realize that they're in a kind of a special category. They're a race apart. They're no longer Mr and Mrs Smith, a couple with a grown-up family, but two people who've joined the ranks of the drop-outs, the problem people, the 'senior citizens' as they choose to call them. But the old people don't call themselves the senior citizens – they call themselves the second-class citizens.

How can they be other than second-class citizens surrounded as they are by people all like themselves, all old, all living in the same road or block and all with the same problems and the same incomes? How much better it would be if the old were mixed up with the young. Most neighbours feel kindly towards elderly people, especially elderly people who are not capable of getting out themselves. They'd help in so many small ways. Carry coal, do a bit of shopping and explain the forms that they get sent and that simply plague them.

Another thing that neighbours could do is to persuade some of those who are living on a pittance to accept social security. It's amazing the number of old people that won't take social security. They look on it as their parents looked on the old parish relief. My mother remembers it well – when the authority used to come round, open all your cupboards to see how much food you had and tell you what they thought you could do without. Then any furniture that they didn't consider you needed they told you to sell it before you asked for money. It isn't anything like that now. They help old people as unobtrusively as they can. They make you feel that it's not a charity but a right.

Another type of old person I feel particularly sorry for is what I think they call 'distressed gentlefolk'. Mind you, I suffered at the hands of gentlefolk when I was in service, but that's forgotten now. One of these ladies said to me, 'It's the cold winters I worry about – you see I can't afford much coal and it makes all the difference to being up and around or staying in bed all the time.' When I asked her what she missed most from the comfortable life that she used to have she said, 'Most of all I miss not being able to afford a private doctor.' And I felt a fellow feeling with her because that is one of the things I would like. She said, 'I never go to the doctor now unless I've really got to. There's four doctors in a group practice where I am registered and I hardly ever get the same one twice so I've got to explain my symptoms each time I go. While I'm doing this he's writing on a pad and when I've finished he just hands me a prescription without a word and out I go. I'm sure all the doctors in that group favour contraceptives for the unmarried, abortions for the married and euthanasia for the unwanted like me.'

She herself believed in euthanasia.

She said, 'I consider that when we become a misery to ourselves and our relations we should have the privilege of removing ourselves from life if we want to.'

I think I agree with her. Old age can be, and should be, a time of gracious living and companionship. But it can also be a time of loneliness and wretchedness. There's precious little dignity about coming into the world so let us at least leave it in the best possible way that we can.

20

DIGNITY WAS SOMETHING that in my early life the working classes were not supposed to be able to afford.

As a kitchenmaid I was at everyone's beck and call and the kind of work I was doing meant that I always looked scruffy. So I felt what I was called, a skivvy, and feeling like this gave me an inferiority complex, or what we call today a chip on my shoulder.

When I was going out I would make what I thought was the best of myself but that was only my opinion at the time, and looking back on it my opinion must often have been wrong. Of privacy we had none. Working and sharing a bedroom as I did meant I was never alone; my life was what you would call an open book. I don't think I resented this at the time – open book it might have been but it wasn't a very interesting one.

But dignity and privacy are two things that I have since thought go side by side. So when I saw how more and more country houses were being opened to the general public I wondered how their owners felt about this invasion into their lives.

I knew of course that their education had prepared them to meet any situation but I wondered – if they showed any emotion – whether their feelings were the same as mine.

It was with a very strange sensation and a not altogether agreeable one that I went to Woburn Abbey to interview the Duke of Bedford for the BBC. Although during my years in domestic service I'd never worked in such a grand establishment, nevertheless for me to go in at the front door instead of the basement and talk to the owner – well, it was something I never thought would happen, not in my wildest dreams. In domestic service the only time you ever went in by the front door was when you went after the job, never for the rest of your time there did you ever sully it except by cleaning it.

I had read about the Duke, how he was sociable and happy-go-lucky, but that didn't mean a thing to me because people that are sociable and happy-go-lucky were, in my experience, only sociable and happy-go-lucky to people of their own class. The sociability and affability got shed like a snake skin when they were dealing with what they designated the lower classes. So I thought, maybe he is all they crack him up to be but if he knows what I was originally he won't be the same to me. So I felt a bit nervous at the thought of the coming interview.

But I must say His Grace surprised me. He was not a bit like I expected. On the contrary he made me feel as though I was really welcome. He chatted me up over a glass of

MARGARET POWELL

sherry. And his comments on his ancestors were witty and often far from flattering. I mean describing some he said 'the only sensible thing they'd ever done was to marry money'. And then he went on to describe the things that some of the others had done which were unprintable. So I felt at my ease from the start instead of feeling that I'd got to be on the defensive all the time. By defensive I mean I went there all tensed up, ready to be aggressive if I felt that he was going to talk down at me. I thought: 'Never mind, just because I've been in domestic service, I'm not working for him so I haven't got to be feeling as though he's "Sir" to me. Naturally I'll give him his title. But he needn't think that I'm going to be subservient. Jack's as good as his master.' I know he isn't really but then I always sort of build myself up with the fact that he is, you see.

But he took the wind right out of my sails and so did his house – it was absolutely wonderful. I still think about it now, that marvellous place. It was full of the most beautiful things, and as he took me around I realized the deep feelings the Duke had in owning them. I've never felt any desire to own things, even valuable things, but I sensed that he looked at them as something in trust from his family. He hadn't actually bought them for himself and he was honouring that trust by his determination to keep them.

I began to realize more how one does feel towards really beautiful though inanimate things. We've got nothing in our house that the dustman would give us twopence for – it's all utility stuff, stuff you can't really feel a pride in, and the house is just a place where we live and that's all you can say about it. But that house was where other people had lived and the things in it were things they'd used and loved and it needed very little imagination to visualize what it must have been like when they were used to the full, when it wasn't just a place where a small part was used by the family and the rest had to be thrown open for every Tom, Dick, and Harry who cared to fork out half a crown to come round and stare at. I could visualize, having been in domestic service, the large parties and balls that were given there and the rank and nobility that attended them.

All right, they'd never done a stroke of work in their lives but I could forgive them that. I could see them under the chandeliers and walking down the staircases. And now these things were just there for people to stare at. But it was good to feel they were all in use at one time, that they had to be kept clean by servants, that they weren't always show pieces.

I thought what a retinue of servants they must have had below stairs to wait hand and foot on those people above. And I was glad that there were lovely houses like that even though I didn't admire them when I was working. I'm glad too that they are open to the public to see. It's not the same thing reading about them as being able to visit them.

Nevertheless, I felt a kind of discomfort going round Woburn Abbey. It seemed an invasion of people's privacy, that my strange eyes should peer at things that the Duke's grandmothers and great-grandmothers and great-great-grandmothers had loved, used, and handled. I was violating these things with my eyes. Maybe the Duke doesn't feel like that but I did. That I really shouldn't be there – peering into private places because through force of circumstances or economic or political pressure they're no longer able to be kept in peace. When I look at lovely things, see them in a home and part of a home, they take on a far more personal and appealing appearance than they do in a museum. Museums are soulless places.

And then there's the Duke of Bedford not only enjoying taking me round but talking about other visitors that he liked sharing his possessions with. He didn't feel that fate had dealt him a harsh blow in any way. He really seemed to enjoy the fact that he could share them and that it was by people's half-crowns that he was able to keep the whole thing going. He thought, it's just one of those things and that all the stately-home owners were in the same boat and that it was far better than having to give them up altogether.

Although he spoke in a flippant way, too, about his ancestors, I don't really think he felt flippant. Perhaps to people whom he must realize have got no ancestors they want to acknowledge it's just as well to be flippant, particularly about those you've got hanging on your walls, unless you want to hear some peculiar remarks. None of my ancestors would I ever want hanging on walls, I can assure you. But then I don't come from the line of stately homes.

Anyway during this personally conducted tour His Grace certainly was lighthearted. He wasn't in any way condescending. Of course I was interested in the mechanics of throwing a stately home open to the public – how it was kept clean? What kind of floor covering they had? And he described the kind of material which was the most hard wearing. Then he told me he had a dozen or more people coming in from the village every day to dust – thank heaven I wasn't one of them! I'd have been frightened to pick up anything, let alone put a duster around it.

And it isn't only the house. The Duke of Bedford's got a lot of outside attractions as well. You might say he's an impresario; he believes in giving value for money. Some owners consider they're doing a great service by allowing the public to see how the wealthy live. For half a crown you see them in the lap of luxury then you can go back home and have a big moan about bloated aristocrats. You've got ammunition for your gun, haven't you?

At some of these stately homes you get a sort of potted history lesson while they take you round. I was glad the Duke didn't because history as presented by people whose ancestors have lived it on the upper level is not the same as the history you read. Give me the Industrial Revolution and the poor old down-trodden working class of the Victorian days, that's the kind of thing I like, not how well the wealthy lived.

Then you get other stately-home owners who light-heartedly say there's nothing to being a lord. In fact if you read some of the remarks of the aristocracy you would think that they feel that there's a sort of special privilege in being a non-privileged person. It's a kind of inverted snobbery. But the great British public love them, otherwise they'd get rid of the House of Lords.

I think it's an anomaly. One peer even had the nerve to

say that the House of Lords was the last bulwark against democracy. What he meant by that I don't know, but it sounds pretty inflammatory. I reckon it's the working class that need the aristocracy; we have got something to fight against. So keep them there and keep up the struggle. We must continue to fight for the fact all men are equal regardless that some of course will always be more equal than others.

All the time I was going round Woburn Abbey these thoughts were going through my head. The interview went well, largely because His Grace made it all so easy. We talked in his private sitting-room. Afterwards I happened to notice one of the oil paintings on the wall, a Rembrandt it was, the companion picture to one that had recently been auctioned and sold for three-quarters of a million pounds.

When the Duke told me this I said, 'And is that one worth that much?'

'Yes,' he said, 'I should think so – possibly a little more.'

So I said, 'Well, why don't you sell it?'

'Oh, I don't know,' he said, 'it looks rather cosy up there don't you think?'

Cosy! I ask you. But after that remark I thought perhaps we'd better keep the House of Lords after all.

Then he delivered his *coup de grâce* which showed me that I'm the same sort of snob as all of them. As we got up to leave, to my amazement he said, 'But surely you're staying for lunch?' And to my absolute astonishment and fury the producer said, 'I'm very sorry, we really haven't time. We've got to get this tape to the BBC. It goes out this evening.'

I nearly died with mortification when I heard him say this because to have been able to have gone back to my home and said to my neighbours in the course of conversation, 'When I had lunch with the Duke of Bedford,' you can imagine what that would have done for me. It was no good saying, 'The day the Duke of Bedford asked me to lunch.' I mean, the idea that I'd refuse! As we drove back home in silence, because I wasn't speaking to the producer by then, I thought of the number of things that would have reminded me of the day I had lunch with the Duke of Bedford. Then it struck me what the Duke had done for me. He showed me that in spite of all my talk about 'them up there and us below stairs,' if one can possibly associate with them, one does so – which makes us all really snobs at heart, or perhaps just ordinary mortals.

www.panmacmillan.com